Spotlight on Young Children

Challenging Behavior

Charis L. Wahman & Janice K. Lee EDITORS

National Association for the Education of Young Children
Washington, DC

National Association for the Education of Young Children

1401 H Street NW, Suite 600
Washington, DC 20005
202-232-8777 • 800-424-2460
NAEYC.org

NAEYC Books

**Senior Director, Publishing
& Content Development**
Susan Friedman

Director, Books
Dana Battaglia

Senior Editor
Holly Bohart

Editor II
Rossella Procopio

Senior Creative Design Manager
Charity Coleman

Senior Creative Design Specialist
Gillian Frank

**Publishing Business
Operations Manager**
Francine Markowitz

Through its publications program, the National Association for the Education of Young Children (NAEYC) provides a forum for discussion of major issues and ideas in the early childhood field, with the hope of provoking thought and promoting professional growth. The views expressed or implied in this book are not necessarily those of the Association.

Contents

Introduction

Charis L. Wahman and Janice K. Lee

Stacey, a new preschool teacher, looks around the room as the children transition from morning group time to center activities. She feels flustered and overwhelmed. David has fallen on the floor, kicking and screaming as he reaches to take his favorite truck from a peer. Charlotte yells loudly while flinging a red paintbrush across the morning carpet. Phillip runs away from the adults to the classroom sink to play "splash" and dumps a bucket of water onto the floor. A few children giggle, pushing and pulling each other around the carpet. Stacey stands up, places her hands on her hips, and lets out a big sigh. Her coteacher's expression displays equal feelings of exasperation.

Later in the afternoon while the children are napping, Stacey reflects on the morning's events and asks herself a number of questions. What are the behaviors that are most challenging to her and the other staff? What is the most efficient way they could prevent those behaviors from occurring? How can she teach skills that meet different needs across specific routines and activities? How might she support the children in her classroom who demonstrate persistent challenging behavior? And what self-care strategies can she put in place to keep herself going each day?

Addressing young children's challenging behavior is a daily practical concern for teachers like Stacey, and it has long been a primary concern within the field of early childhood education (NRC & IOM 2000). *Challenging behavior*—that is, "any repeated pattern of behavior, or perception of behavior, that interferes with or is at risk of interfering with optimal learning or engagement in prosocial interactions with peers and adults" (Smith & Fox 2003, 6)—is not uncommon. Although few studies have addressed overall prevalence, it has been estimated that roughly 10 to 14 percent of children from birth to 5 years old demonstrate serious behavioral concerns (Brauner & Stephens 2006). This percentage is likely to increase given the increasing numbers of children with adverse childhood experiences and/or disabilities entering early learning environments (Giovanelli et al. 2020; Lipscomb et al. 2021; NCES 2023) and the residual impact of the COVID-19 pandemic on young children's social and emotional well-being (Sun et al. 2022; Weiland et al. 2021).

Early childhood educators should *expect* challenging behavior from young children based on their current development (Denham 2018). Young children have not yet been taught appropriate behavior, and teaching approaches and practices should integrate this understanding (Hemmeter & Conroy 2018). Cultivating relationally safe environments is a fundamental approach to addressing young children's challenging behavior. Nevertheless, many early childhood educators struggle to address the behavioral needs of young children, and children who have experienced toxic stress or have disabilities are especially likely to face punishment and exclusionary discipline practices, including suspension and expulsion (OCR 2021; Zeng et al. 2019).

Exclusionary discipline causes lasting harm to children and their families (Doubet & Ostrosky 2015; Wahman et al. 2022). These practices, which are largely used in reaction to externalized challenging behavior (e.g., aggression, tantrums, noncompliance) and often impacted by implicit biases (Okonofua & Eberhardt 2015), do not provide children with access, participation, or supports (DEC & NAEYC 2009). Furthermore, use of exclusionary discipline practices in early learning programs correlates with an increased likelihood that children will be suspended or expelled again, drop out of high school, experience academic failure, and have contact with the criminal justice system (Stegelin 2018). The disproportionate impact of preschool suspension and expulsion on Black and Latino/a children (Gilliam et al. 2016; Meek et al. 2020) and children with disabilities (Novoa & Malik 2018) is another indication that teachers are inadequately prepared to meet the behavioral needs of young children and need systematic supports (Hoffman & Kuvalanka 2019).

Early childhood professionals trained in high-quality social and emotional practices use approaches based on an understanding of *why* a challenging behavior occurs. They implement responsive interactions, such as building trust and connections with children, identifying appropriate skills the child can use instead of the challenging behavior, and supporting teachers and families in implementing effective teaching strategies for those skills (Garrity et al. 2019). Evidence-based social and emotional interventions can serve as a protective factor for children, particularly for those experiencing adverse circumstances, because children learn skills that help them navigate stressful experiences (Austin, Lesak, & Shanahan 2020; Hemmeter & Conroy 2018).

Recognizing the importance of responsive frameworks and the detrimental impact of exclusionary discipline on young children, the US Department of Health and Human Services (HHS) and the US Department of Education (ED; 2014) released a joint policy statement with the goal of preventing suspension and expulsion and highlighting evidence-based positive behavior intervention and support strategies. Over 30 organizations signed a statement in collective support of these recommendations (NAEYC 2017). Recently, a more updated version of the policy statement was released (HHS & ED 2023). Decades of research have documented the positive effects of tiered prevention frameworks on children's behavioral outcomes (see, e.g., Fox, Strain, & Dunlap 2021; Hemmeter et al. 2016; Horner, Sugai, & Anderson 2010). For example, the multi-tiered system of supports (MTSS), drawn from a public health model, organizes strategies to help adults provide increasing levels of support for children (universal, targeted, and individualized).

Importantly, implementation of a tiered prevention framework using a team-based approach with early childhood educators, families, and related service personnel provides a more robust response system for intervention. These intervention practices include designing relationally safe and nurturing environments, partnering with families and school teams, social and emotional skill building, planned systematic instruction, and adapting practices to consider the cultures and contexts of children (Fox, Strain, & Dunlap 2021).

This volume brings together articles that highlight these strategies and further address topics for the field to promote evidence-based supports for young children with challenging behavior. The articles are grouped into three parts, each focusing on a different tier common to well-established and widely used social and emotional learning frameworks (e.g., Fox et al. 2003):

> Part One: Preventive Practices

> Part Two: Targeted Practices

> Part Three: Intensive and Individualized Practices

Notably, each of the articles in this volume takes a strong stance against the use of punishment as discipline and advocates for approaches that encourage relationship-building and teaching children skills to decrease challenging behavior. The articles are accompanied by questions that promote reflection and application.

Many children and their families enter early learning environments with stories of survival. As you read these articles, consider your role in fostering healing-centered classrooms and how these practices honor the humanity in young children, center their voices, and allow them to be fully seen and heard.

REFERENCES

Austin, A.E., A.M. Lesak, & M.E. Shanahan. 2020. "Risk and Protective Factors for Child Maltreatment: A Review." *Current Epidemiology Reports* 7 (4): 334–42.

Brauner, C.B., & C.B. Stephens. 2006. "Estimating the Prevalence of Early Childhood Serious Emotional/Behavioral Disorders: Challenges and Recommendations." *Public Health Reports* 121 (3): 303–10.

DEC (Division for Early Childhood) & NAEYC. 2009. "Early Childhood Inclusion." Joint position statement. Chapel Hill: The University of North Carolina, FPG Child Development Institute. www.naeyc.org/files/naeyc/file/positions/DEC_NAEYC_EC_updatedKS.pdf.

Denham, S.A. 2018. "Keeping SEL Developmental: The Importance of a Developmental Lens for Fostering and Assessing SEL Competencies." *Measuring SEL: Using Data to Inspire Practice (Frameworks Briefs)*. Chicago: CASEL. https://measuringsel.casel.org/wp-content/uploads/2018/11/Frameworks-DevSEL.pdf.

Doubet, S.L., & M.M. Ostrosky. 2015. "The Impact of Challenging Behavior on Families: I Don't Know What to Do." *Topics in Early Childhood Special Education* 34 (4): 223–33.

Fox, L., G. Dunlap, M.L. Hemmeter, G.E. Joseph, & P.S. Strain. 2003. "The Teaching Pyramid: A Model for Supporting Social Competence and Preventing Challenging Behavior in Young Children." *Young Children* 58 (4): 48–52.

Fox, L., P.S. Strain, & G. Dunlap. 2021. "Preventing the Use of Preschool Suspension and Expulsion: Implementing the Pyramid Model." *Preventing School Failure: Alternative Education for Children and Youth* 65 (4): 312–22.

Garrity, S.M., S.L. Longstreth, L.K. Linder, & N. Salcedo Potter. 2019. "Early Childhood Education Centre Director Perceptions of Challenging Behavior: Promising Practices and Implications for Professional Development." *Children & Society* 33 (2): 168–84.

Gilliam, W.S., A.N. Maupin, C.R. Reyes, M. Accavitti, & F. Shic. 2016. "Do Early Educators' Implicit Biases Regarding Sex and Race Relate to Behavior Expectations and Recommendations of Preschool Expulsions and Suspensions?" *Yale University Child Study Center* 9 (28): 1–16.

Giovanelli, A., C.F. Mondi, A.J. Reynolds, & S.R. Ou. 2020. "Adverse Childhood Experiences: Mechanisms of Risk and Resilience in a Longitudinal Urban Cohort." *Development and Psychopathology* 32 (4): 1418–39.

Hemmeter, M.L., & M.A. Conroy. 2018. "Advancement of Evidence-Based Programs for Young Children with Social and Emotional Learning Difficulties." *School Mental Health* 10: 199–201.

Hemmeter, M.L., P. Snyder, L. Fox, & J. Algina. 2016. "The Efficacy of the Pyramid Model: Effects on Teachers, Classrooms, and Children." *Topics in Early Childhood Special Education* 36: 133–46.

HHS (US Department of Health and Human Services) & ED (US Department of Education). 2014. "Policy Statement on Expulsion and Suspension Policies in Early Childhood Settings." Washington, DC: HHS & ED. https://oese.ed.gov/files/2020/07/policy-statement-ece-expulsions-suspensions.pdf.

HHS & ED. 2023. "Policy Statement on Inclusion of Children with Disabilities in Early Childhood Programs." Washington, DC: HHS & ED. https://sites.ed.gov/idea/idea-files/policy-statement-inclusion-of-children-with-disabilities-in-early-childhood-programs.

Hoffman, T.K., & K.A. Kuvalanka. 2019. "Behavior Problems in Child Care Classrooms: Insights from Child Care Teachers." *Preventing School Failure: Alternative Education for Children and Youth* 63 (3): 259–68.

Horner, R.H., G. Sugai, & C.M. Anderson. 2010. "Examining the Evidence Base for School-Wide Positive Behavior Support." *Focus on Exceptional Children* 42 (8): 1–14.

Lipscomb, S.T., B. Hatfield, H. Lewis, E. Goka-Dubose, & C. Abshire. 2021. "Adverse Childhood Experiences and Children's Development in Early Care and Education Programs." *Journal of Applied Developmental Psychology* 72: 101218.

Meek, S., L. Smith, R. Allen, E. Catherine, K. Edyburn, C. Williams, R. Fabes, K. McIntosh, E. Garcia, R. Takanishi, L. Gordon, O. Jimenez-Castellanos, M.L. Hemmeter, W. Gilliam, & R. Pontier. 2020. "Start with Equity: From the Early Years to the Early Grades." Tempe: Arizona State University Children's Equity Project and Bipartisan Policy Center. https://childandfamilysuccess.asu.edu/sites/default/files/2020-07/CEP-report-071520-FINAL.pdf.

NAEYC. 2017. "Standing Together Against Suspension and Expulsion in Early Childhood." Joint statement. Washington, DC: NAEYC. www.naeyc.org/sites/default/files/globally-shared/downloads/PDFs/resources/topics/Standing%20Together.Joint%20Statement.FINAL__9_0.pdf.

NCES (National Center for Education Statistics, Institute of Education Sciences, US Department of Education). 2023. "Students with Disabilities." *Condition of Education*, last modified May 1. https://nces.ed.gov/programs/coe/indicator/cgg.

Novoa, C., & R. Malik. 2018. *Suspensions Are Not Support: The Disciplining of Preschoolers with Disabilities*. Report. Washington, DC: Center for American Progress. www.americanprogress.org/article/suspensions-not-support.

NRC (National Research Council) & IOM (Institute of Medicine). 2000. *From Neurons to Neighborhoods: The Science of Early Childhood Development*. Report. Washington, DC: National Academies Press.

OCR (Office for Civil Rights, US Department of Education). 2021. "An Overview of Exclusionary Discipline Practices in Public Schools for the 2017–18 School Year." https://ocrdata.ed.gov/assets/downloads/crdc-exclusionary-school-discipline.pdf.

Okonofua, J.A., & J.L. Eberhardt. 2015. "Two Strikes: Race and the Disciplining of Young Students." *Psychological Science* 26 (5): 617–24.

Smith, B., & L. Fox. 2003. *Systems of Service Delivery: A Synthesis of Evidence Relevant to Young Children at Risk of or Who Have Challenging Behavior*. Tampa, FL: Center for Evidence-Based Practice: Young Children with Challenging Behavior.

Sun, J., B. Singletary, H. Jiang, L.M. Justice, T.-J. Lin, & K.M. Purtell. 2022. "Child Behavior Problems During COVID-19: Associations with Parent Distress and Child Social-Emotional Skills." *Journal of Applied Developmental Psychology* 78 (Jan-Feb): 101375.

Stegelin, D.A. 2018. "Preschool Suspension and Expulsion: Defining the Issues." Brief. Greenville, SC: Institute for Child Success. www.instituteforchildsuccess.org/wp-content/uploads/2018/12/ICS-2018-PreschoolSuspensionBrief-WEB.pdf.

Wahman, C.L., T. Steele, E.A. Steed, & L. Powers. 2022. "No Intervention, Just Straight Suspension: Family Perspectives of Suspension and Expulsion." *Children and Youth Services Review* 143 (December): 106678.

Weiland, C., E. Greenberg, D. Bassok, A. Markowitz, P.G. Rosada, G. Luetmer, R. Abenavoli, C. Gomez, A. Johnson, B. Jones-Harden, M. Maier, M. McCormick, P. Morris, M. Nores, D. Phillips, & C. Snow. 2021. "Historic Crisis, Historic Opportunity: Using Evidence to Mitigate the Effects of the COVID-19 Crisis on Young Children and Early Care and Education Programs." Brief. Ann Arbor: University of Michigan Education Policy Initiative. https://edpolicy.umich.edu/sites/epi/files/2021-07/EPI-UI-Covid%20Synthesis%20Brief%20June%202021.pdf.

Zeng, S., C.P. Corr, C. O'Grady, & Y. Guan. 2019. "Adverse Childhood Experiences and Preschool Suspension Expulsion: A Population Study." *Child Abuse and Neglect* 97: 104149.

About the Editors

Charis L. Wahman, PhD, BCBA-D, is assistant professor of special education at Michigan State University. She also serves as a clinician in early care settings to support young children with social and emotional needs. Charis has conducted research, published articles, and presented on the social and emotional development of young children and families' experiences with suspension and expulsion at national conferences.

Janice K. Lee, PhD, BCBA, is state coordinator for the Nevada Pyramid Model Partnership through the University of Nevada, Reno. In addition to conducting research and publishing articles on the pyramid model, she also provides training, coaching, consultation, and technical assistance on social and emotional skill development to teachers, practitioners, and families to prevent and address challenging behavior.

Preventive Practices

An old adage says, "you cannot give what you do not have." Teachers experiencing stress and burnout are less responsive to young children's social and emotional development (Jeon et al. 2019). One fundamental aspect of preventive practices is that nurturing your own well-being enhances your capacity to care for children. Preventive practices also focus on building positive connections with all children, adapting strategies that consider the cultures and characteristics of children and their families, and attending to the environment to ensure that each of these practices are embedded across routines and transitions. With these goals, teachers nurture an environment that fosters relational healing, encourages positive behavior, and prevents challenging behavior from occurring.

The five articles in this part provide teachers with concrete strategies and examples for how to implement preventive practices in the classroom.

Katherine M. Zinsser, Susanne A. Denham, and **Timothy W. Curby** describe social and emotional learning as an ongoing process of reflection, knowledge, and awareness. Their article, "Becoming a Social and Emotional Teacher: The Heart of Good Guidance," shows how teachers learn through intrapersonal and interpersonal relationships to take care of themselves physically and emotionally while also learning to connect with children who may demonstrate comfortable (positive) or uncomfortable (negative) emotions.

In "Culturally Responsive Strategies to Support Young Children with Challenging Behavior," **Charis L. Wahman** and **Elizabeth A. Steed** share five strategies that promote positive teacher-child relationships, a core preventive practice that moderates the risk of early school failure for children with challenging behavior.

Similarly, **Zeynep Isik-Ercan** discusses the cultural appropriateness of children's behavior across routines. "Culturally Appropriate Positive Guidance with Young Children" also explores how to identify learning opportunities for children through healthy partnerships with families.

In "Understanding Young Children's Play: Seeing Behavior Through the Lens of Attachment Theory," **Shulamit N. Riblatt** and **Sascha Longstreth** share how to build important relationships with children through play interactions.

A playground offers time and space for active, engaged play, but this setting is also ripe for challenging behavior. In "Outdoor Recess Matters! Preventing and Reducing Children's Challenging Behavior on the Playground," **Hsiu-Wen Yang, Michaelene M. Ostrosky, Paddy Cronin Favazza, Yusuf Akemoğlu, W. Catherine Cheung,** and **Katherine Aronson-Ensign** describe how to design universal supports to prevent and reduce challenging behavior during outside play time.

REFERENCE

Jeon, L., C.K. Buettner, A.A. Grant, & S.N. Lang. 2019. "Early Childhood Teachers' Stress and Children's Social, Emotional, and Behavioral Functioning." *Journal of Applied Developmental Psychology* 61 (March–April): 21–32.

Becoming a Social and Emotional Teacher

The Heart of Good Guidance

Katherine M. Zinsser, Susanne A. Denham, and Timothy W. Curby

It's the end of center time, and Jerome is standing beside the preschool classroom's computer screaming, "I want to play!" His teacher, Ms. Carolyn, crosses the room and squats beside him. She says, "I know that game is really fun, but you've already had your computer time this morning. See the center chart? Now it's José's turn. You can watch him play, but you'll have to wait to play again."

Jerome scowls at Ms. Carolyn, balls up his fists and slams them down on the keyboard in front of José, yelling, "I want to play NOW!" Ms. Carolyn takes a deep breath to remain calm. She has been working with Jerome on managing and expressing his feelings, and she reflects briefly on the strategies that have worked in the past.

"Jerome," Ms. Carolyn says, "it looks like you're having a really big feeling right now, and that's okay. But it's not okay for you to hurt our classroom materials or to yell like that because it hurts your friends' ears—and mine." Ms. Carolyn shows Jerome her slightly sad facial expression and asks, "Do you remember our calm-down song? Do you want to sing it with me?"

Ms. Carolyn begins singing, "Take three deep breaths" and places her hands on her stomach as she takes a deep breath. Hesitantly, Jerome joins in, singing quietly at first but matching her hand gestures and breathing: "Now count to three, 1-2-3, calm down, calm down."

Ms. Carolyn's reaction to Jerome's outburst helped to promote his social and emotional learning. In fact, her behaviors could be described as social and emotional teaching. Each of her actions—coming to Jerome when he was upset, remaining calm in a stressful situation, displaying an appropriate emotional reaction (sadness) when Jerome yelled, connecting Jerome's emotions with the curriculum used in her classroom, and modeling an appropriate way to handle strong feelings—are teaching Jerome about the social and emotional world.

The term *social and emotional learning* is often used in early childhood education settings to encompass the behavioral and emotional skills children will need to be ready for kindergarten. However, it is important for teachers to keep in mind that social and emotional learning is an ongoing process of acquiring a set of skills or competencies, not the skills themselves. In early childhood, this process is grounded in the relationships children have with their caregivers.

In addition to parents, teachers play a critical role in the process through *social and emotional teaching*. Such teaching goes beyond direct instruction and related curricular programs; it is highly dependent on teachers' own social and emotional skills. In this article, we synthesize recent research in child development and early childhood education to describe how teachers can foster social and emotional learning through their everyday interactions with preschool-aged children.

Before defining the components of effective social and emotional teaching, it is important to first consider what competencies teachers may wish to promote in young children for social and academic success. These interrelated abilities include

> **Being socially and emotionally aware:** the ability to identify one's own and others' emotions as well as empathize with someone, even when you feel differently than they do. *Aaron knew that Chantel was crying and felt sad because another child refused to let her play at the water table.*

> **Regulating one's emotions:** the ability to manage one's emotions and behaviors across various situations. *Martin laughed and danced across the carpet during music time but knew to be "quiet as a mouse" when walking in the hallway.*

> **Making socially responsible decisions:** the ability to consider social norms and the consequences of one's actions when making decisions about how to behave. *Jessica felt really mad when Andre accidentally bumped her block tower and sent it tumbling to the floor. But she could tell by looking at Andre's surprised face that he didn't mean to, so instead of yelling or throwing the blocks, she asked if he would help her build it again.*

Children who are more skilled in these areas have more success making friends, are more positive about school, and have better grades later in elementary school (Denham, Brown, & Domitrovich 2010). The academic benefits of social and emotional learning make sense when you consider the competing emotional and attentional demands on preschoolers in busy, productive classrooms. The related concepts of social and emotional competence, self-regulation, and executive function are often grouped by researchers under the umbrella of *learning-related skills* (McClelland et al. 2007), which all contribute to children's social and academic achievement.

Social and Emotional Teaching

Children develop social and emotional skills primarily through interactions with family members, teachers, and peers. With many children spending large amounts of time in preschool (and other early education) settings, the influence of early childhood teachers on children's social and emotional learning is attracting greater attention. Across the country, teachers are held accountable by early learning standards to promote their students' social and emotional skills—but until recently, it was unclear what sorts of social and emotional teaching practices are highly effective.

Teachers promote social and emotional learning through a variety of activities and practices, some purposeful and planned, some naturally occurring. By reviewing the research, observing teacher-child interactions, and interviewing practitioners, we developed a model for social and emotional teaching with four essential components: (1) using a curriculum that addresses a broad range of social and emotional skills; (2) being a socially and emotionally competent teacher; (3) capitalizing on everyday interactions as natural opportunities for social and emotional learning; and (4) creating a positive emotional climate in the classroom. Together, as explained throughout the rest of this article, these practices facilitate the learning process, helping children acquire and practice using social and emotional competencies.

Using a Social and Emotional Learning Curriculum

Research has shown that high-quality social and emotional curricula can improve children's skills in the short and long terms (Bierman & Motamedi 2015; Domitrovich, Cortes, & Greenberg 2007; Durlak et al. 2011). When teachers use a research-based curriculum effectively, they provide students opportunities to develop foundational skills—such as being able to identify and label their own and others' emotions—that support later academic performance, school adjustment, peer relationships, and overall emotional well-being. The CASEL (2012) guide, *Effective Social and Emotional Learning Programs*, identifies seven evidence-based preschool programs that successfully promote children's self-control, relationship building, and problem solving, among other social and emotional skills. Administrators and teachers may find guides such as this one helpful in identifying and selecting evidence-based programs (see https://pg.casel.org for more information).

Although direct social and emotional instruction through curriculum can be effective, teachers should not limit their instruction to the prescribed lessons or feel confined by the curriculum (Zinsser et al. 2014). The three remaining components of our social and emotional teaching model work in conjunction with high-quality curricula to enhance children's learning.

Being a Socially and Emotionally Competent Teacher

Just as children come to school each day with their emotions, experiences, and backgrounds, teachers also differ in how successfully they navigate their social and emotional lives. These differences have meaningful impacts on how easily teachers can help children with social and emotional learning. When teachers experience, regulate, and appropriately express their emotions—positive or negative—in the classroom, they are modeling for children the social norms associated with different feelings and how to communicate those feelings. Teachers' positive displays of warmth, joy, and excitement can positively impact children's emotional well-being and promote learning (Ahn & Stifter 2006). Conversely, teachers' displays of negative emotions in the classroom—especially when frequent, not well regulated, and not moderated for an audience of young learners—are associated with children's poorer emotion regulation and increased aggressive behaviors (Ramsden & Hubbard 2002).

Teachers who are more aware of and knowledgeable about emotions may more easily scaffold children's labeling of emotions and empathize with their complex emotional experiences. Teachers who are successful at regulating their emotions may respond to challenging interactions with students in more effective ways. For example, if Mr. Diego needs to help Suzie through a temper tantrum, he may regulate his own frustration, choose to validate Suzie's expression, and help her problem solve. Mr. Diego might say, "I see that you're very upset because you can't play in the block area right now. Is there somewhere else you would like to play while you wait?" Knowing that Suzie enjoys the water table, he may also help her redirect her energy and reconsider her reaction: "Suzie, the water table is available. Would you like to play there with me while you calm down?" Once they are playing quietly together, Mr. Diego may find natural opportunities to reinforce that Suzie can have fun even while waiting for her preferred activity to become available.

Similarly, teachers who are better able to manage their emotions (thereby generally staying on an even keel in the classroom) can create a consistently positive emotional environment. Children learn what to expect from their teacher and anticipate that the teacher will respond to their emotional expressions with understanding, further supporting children's learning process (Zinsser et al. 2013). In contrast, teachers' negative feelings—including frustration, annoyance, and boredom—may detract from their ability to engage in effective social and emotional teaching. Teachers who experience intense negative emotions at work, such as stress or depression, are more likely to frequently express negative emotions and to react punitively to children's expression of emotions (Ersay 2007).

When teachers invest in developing their social and emotional competencies and take proactive steps to reduce their stress and regulate their emotions (both in and outside of the classroom), they not only feel better about themselves but may also be more effective social and emotional teachers (Zinsser et al. 2013). For steps teachers can take, see "Tips for Advancing Your Social and Emotional Competence."

Tips for Advancing Your Social and Emotional Competence

There are many small steps you can take to build your competence and enhance your social and emotional teaching.

> **Take care of yourself.** Your physical and emotional health are critical! Studies show that meditation and mindfulness classes can decrease teachers' experiences of stress and burnout (Buchanan 2017). Check out the Association for Mindfulness in Education: www.mindfuleducation.org.

> **Practice what you preach.** Adopt a few routines and strategies for regulating your negative emotions when they arise at work or at home. Maybe start with the simple ones you want your students to use (e.g., take a deep breath, count to three).

> **Examine your work environment.** What can you do to make your classroom a positive (frustration-free) place to work, learn, and play? The National Center for Pyramid Model Innovations suggests several simple tips: www.challengingbehavior.org/resources.

> **Don't go it alone.** Successful social and emotional teaching and learning require integrated support at all levels. Seek out mentoring and support from colleagues who will help you reflect on your classroom practice. Building your competencies will take time, so be patient with yourself.

Promoting Social and Emotional Learning Through Interactions

Through their daily interactions, teachers give children information about the nature of various emotions—how, why, and when they are expressed. For example, a teacher may give children information about the individual nature of some emotions, saying, "I scream on roller coasters because the rides scare me, but some people find them fun and laugh instead." Children are constantly observing and processing others' emotional expressions and behaviors and incorporating this learning into their own behavior (Denham, Bassett, & Wyatt 2007). To bring intentionality to this learning through interactions, this component of social and emotional teaching describes how teachers *model* emotional expressions, *teach* about emotions, and *react* to children's emotions.

Teachers' well-regulated, intentional displays of positive and negative emotions are *models* for children of how to convey emotions across a variety of social contexts (Ahn & Stifter 2006). When emotions are expressed clearly, children learn to better recognize emotional expressions (Dunsmore et al. 2009). Similarly, when children see adults modeling appropriate emotional expressions, they develop greater emotion-regulation skills (Eisenberg et al. 2001). At times, teachers can also model the process of identifying and regulating emotions to promote students' use of similar strategies (Zinsser et al. 2015). For example, Ms. Jen may tell her students, "I feel frustrated. I'm going to the calm-down corner to take three deep breaths."

To deepen recognition and understanding of emotions, educators *teach* children the labels, causes, and consequences of emotions through discussions as well as coach children through emotional situations (Denham, Bassett, & Wyatt 2007). Activities like reading stories about feelings can be designed to create opportunities for teachers to directly teach about emotions. Teachers can also capitalize on situations as they arise. For example, following a dispute on the playground, a teacher may scaffold a discussion between the students about each child's emotions and behavioral choices. The teacher might provide labels for children's emotions and suggest strategies to resolve the conflict.

In addition to modeling and teaching, educators should prepare themselves to *react* calmly and supportively to children's emotional displays. Warm, accepting reactions to children's negative emotions—such as sadness and anger—help children better regulate their responses to emotions (Denham, Bassett, & Wyatt 2007). For example, when a teacher crouches down next to a crying child and asks, "What's wrong?" or says, "It's okay to cry when you're sad," they are encouraging a child's expression and validating the emotional experience. Conversely, punitive or dismissive reactions by caregivers are associated with negative outcomes for children (Denham 1998). If a teacher responds to a crying child by saying, "Stop crying! If you keep crying you'll have to go to the baby room," they are belittling a child's emotional experience.

When carefully implemented by a mindful teacher, the components of social and emotional teaching work together. A teacher with strong social and emotional competencies is better able to recognize the origins of a child's negative emotional expressions, to empathize, to regulate their own negative feelings, and to choose a constructive response. In turn, such awareness and sensitivity can strengthen the relationship between the teacher and the child while also enhancing the emotional climate in the classroom.

Creating a Positive Emotional Climate

The emotional climate of an early childhood classroom, which is our final component of social and emotional teaching, is palpable. Markers of positive emotional climates include a classroom feeling warm and inviting, the children appearing comfortable, the teachers enjoying the children's company, and the children and teachers engaging in shared activities (Pianta, La Paro, & Hamre 2008). Such positive learning environments are more enjoyable to spend time in and more conducive to children's social and emotional learning. Children learning in emotionally positive classrooms are more socially competent and display fewer problem behaviors (Mashburn et al. 2008). A positive classroom climate in preschool, in combination with a positive relationship with a preschool teacher, is associated with fewer problem behaviors well into second grade (Howes 2000).

In less positive classrooms, teachers and children may express more negative emotions; there may be power struggles, with teachers relying on raised voices or threats to manage children's behavior. In these classrooms, children tend to rely on more aggressive behaviors directed at peers and teachers to get their needs met. They may also continue to use those troubling strategies into elementary school (Denham et al. 2014).

Although children and teachers cocreate the emotional climate of their classroom, teachers have the advantages of planning and being intentional about the routines they introduce each school year. Teachers also have—or should be striving to develop—the ability to regulate their own emotions and to be mindful of the emotional expression they are modeling for the children. When successfully established, positive classroom climates continue to support social and emotional teaching and learning. Children in classrooms with happier peers have more opportunities to practice positive social skills (Garner 2010), and that practice contributes to an overall positive emotional climate in a classroom. Additionally, working in such positive classrooms may make it easier for teachers to remain happy and engaged in supporting children. If a classroom's climate is generally positive, teachers also have more energy to appropriately manage students' challenging behavior, which otherwise can be a significant contributor to teacher stress and burnout (Hastings & Bham 2003).

Putting the Pieces Together

Social and emotional skills can be learned—and they can be actively taught. While many discussions of children's social and emotional learning focus on teachers' use of specific curricula, teachers support children's development throughout the school day and year in many ways. In addition to using curricula, teachers support the learning process by modeling, teaching, and reacting to emotions and by creating and maintaining consistently positive classroom climates. Furthermore, teachers' effectiveness in using each of these approaches depends, in part,

Reflection Questions

1. What are some steps you can take to be more socially and emotionally aware as a classroom teacher? How might you nurture yourself so you can calmly model and teach social and emotional competencies?

2. How do you and the other adults in your classroom support each other in becoming more socially and emotionally aware? Who do you trust to hold you accountable to growing socially and emotionally, particularly during challenging moments?

3. What brings you joy in your work environment? What challenges you? What are effective ways you've found to work with your emotions in the classroom?

on their own social and emotional competence. By knowing how they can impact their students' social and emotional learning, teachers can extend instruction, guiding children toward competence—and a lifetime of healthy, happy relationships.

REFERENCES

Ahn, H.J., & C. Stifter. 2006. "Child Care Teachers' Response to Children's Emotional Expression." *Early Education and Development* 17 (2): 253–70.

Bierman, K.L., & M. Motamedi. 2015. "Social and Emotional Learning Programs for Preschool Children." Chap. 9 in *Handbook of Social and Emotional Learning: Research and Practice,* eds. J.A. Durlak, C.E. Domitrovich, R.P. Weissberg, & T.P. Gullotta, 135–50. New York: Guilford.

Buchanan, T.K. 2017. "Mindfulness and Meditation in Education." *Young Children* 72 (3): 69–74.

CASEL (Collaborative for Academic, Social, and Emotional Learning). 2012. *2013 CASEL Guide: Effective Social and Emotional Learning Programs—Preschool and Elementary School Edition.* https://files.eric.ed.gov/fulltext/ED581699.pdf

Denham, S.A. 1998. *Emotional Development in Young Children.* Guilford Series on Social and Emotional Development. New York: Guilford.

Denham, S.A., C. Brown, & C.E. Domitrovich. 2010. "'Plays Nice with Others': Social–Emotional Learning and Academic Success." *Early Education and Development* 21 (5): 652–80.

Denham, S.A., H.H. Bassett, K. Zinsser, & T.M. Wyatt. 2014. "How Preschoolers' Social–Emotional Learning Predicts Their Early School Success: Developing Theory-Promoting Competency-Based Assessments." *Infant and Child Development* 23 (4): 426–54.

Denham, S.A., H.H. Bassett, & T.M. Wyatt. 2007. "The Socialization of Emotional Competence." Chap. 24 in *Handbook of Socialization: Theory and Research,* eds. J.E. Grusec & P.D. Hastings, 614–37. New York: Guilford.

Domitrovich, C.E., R.C. Cortes, & M.T Greenberg. 2007. "Improving Young Children's Social and Emotional Competence: A Randomized Trial of the Preschool 'PATHS' Curriculum." *Journal of Primary Prevention* 28 (2): 67–91.

Dunsmore, J.C., P. Her, A.G. Halberstadt, & M.B. Perez-Rivera. 2009. "Parents' Beliefs About Emotions and Children's Recognition of Parents' Emotions." *Journal of Nonverbal Behavior* 33 (2): 121–40.

Durlak, J.A., R.P. Weissberg, A.B. Dymnicki, R.D. Taylor, & K.B. Schellinger. 2011. "The Impact of Enhancing Students' Social and Emotional Learning: A Meta-Analysis of School-Based Universal Interventions." *Child Development* 82 (1): 405–32.

Eisenberg, N., E.T. Gershoff, R.A. Fabes, S.A. Shepard, A.J. Cumberland, S.H. Losoya, I.K. Guthrie, & B.C. Murphy. 2001. "Mother's Emotional Expressivity and Children's Behavior Problems and Social Competence: Mediation Through Children's Regulation." *Developmental Psychology* 37 (4): 475–90.

Ersay, E. 2007. "Preschool Teachers' Emotional Experience Traits, Awareness of Their Own Emotions, and Their Emotional Socialization Practices." PhD diss., Pennsylvania State University.

Garner, P.W. 2010. "Emotional Competence and Its Influences on Teaching and Learning." *Educational Psychology Review* 22 (3): 297–321.

Hastings, R.P., & M.S. Bham. 2003. "The Relationship Between Student Behavior Patterns and Teacher Burnout." *School Psychology International* 24 (1): 115–27.

Howes, C. 2000. "Social-Emotional Classroom Climate in Child Care, Child–Teacher Relationships, and Children's Second Grade Peer Relations." *Social Development* 9 (2): 191–204.

Mashburn, A.J., R.C. Pianta, B.K. Hamre, J.T. Downer, O.A. Barbarin, D. Bryant, M. Burchinal, R. Clifford, D.M. Early, & C. Howes. 2008. "Measures of Classroom Quality in Pre-Kindergarten and Children's Development of Academic, Language, and Social Skills." *Child Development* 79 (3): 732–49.

McClelland, M.M., C.E. Cameron, S.B. Wanless, & A. Murray. 2007. "Executive Function, Behavioral Self-Regulation, and Social-Emotional Competence: Links to School Readiness." Chap. 4 in *Contemporary Perspectives on Social Learning in Early Childhood Education,* eds. O.N. Saracho & B. Spodek, 83–107. Charlotte, NC: Information Age.

Pianta, R.C., K.M. LaParo, & B.K. Hamre. 2008. *Classroom Assessment Scoring System Manual: Pre-K.* Baltimore: Brookes.

Ramsden, S.R., & J.A. Hubbard. 2002. "Family Expressiveness and Parental Emotion Coaching: Their Role in Children's Emotion Regulation and Aggression." *Journal of Abnormal Child Psychology* 30 (6): 657–67.

Zinsser, K.M., C.S. Bailey, T.W. Curby, S.A. Denham, & H.H. Bassett. 2013. "Exploring the Predictable Classroom: Preschool Teacher Stress, Emotional Supportiveness, and Students' Social-Emotional Behavior in Private and Head Start Classrooms." *NHSA Dialog* 16 (2): 90–108.

Zinsser, K.M., E.A. Shewark, S.A. Denham, & T.W. Curby. 2014. "A Mixed-Method Examination of Preschool Teacher Beliefs About Social-Emotional Learning and Relations to Observed Emotional Support." *Infant and Child Development* 23 (5): 471–93.

Zinsser, K.M., S.A. Denham, T.W. Curby, & E.A. Shewark. 2015. "'Practice What You Preach': Teachers' Perceptions of Emotional Competence and Emotionally Supportive Classroom Practices." *Early Education and Development* 26 (7): 899–919.

About the Authors

Katherine M. Zinsser, PhD, is associate professor at the University of Illinois at Chicago, where she conducts applied research to support the social and emotional well-being and development of young children and their caregivers. For resources, visit www.setllab.com.

Susanne A. Denham, PhD, is an applied developmental psychologist and professor emeritus with particular expertise in the social and emotional development of children. In addition to her experience as a mother and grandmother, Susanne also uses her 11 years of hands-on experience as a school psychologist to aid in her research.

Timothy W. Curby, PhD, is professor and interim chair of the Psychology department at George Mason University. Tim's work has focused on understanding the role of teacher-child interactions in promoting children's social, emotional, and academic learning.

Culturally Responsive Strategies to Support Young Children with Challenging Behavior

Charis L. Wahman and Elizabeth A. Steed

Mrs. Green leads the children in her preschool classroom in their morning song: "The more we get together, together, together, the more we get together the hap—." She stops abruptly to run after Miles, who has left morning circle to play with the musical instruments. As Mrs. Green approaches him, Miles folds his arms across his chest, then kicks his legs and screams. Mrs. Green gently places her hand on Miles's arm and looks him in the eye. She says, "Miles, I see that you are upset because you don't want to sit at morning circle and want to play with the musical instruments instead. Should we take the instruments to the circle and play with them after we've finished our calendar activities?" Miles smiles. Mrs. Green notes his response and says, "Okay. First, please sit calmly at morning circle for three minutes; then you can play with the instruments. Is that a deal?" Miles nods. Mrs. Green responds, "Give me a high-five!"

Miles's actions are clearly a source of frustration for his teachers. Although teachers will want to evaluate whether they are planning activities that require children to sit for an extended time and ensure that the activities they offer children are active and meaningful, it is also important for teachers to understand how to support children who exhibit challenging behavior. Challenging behavior is defined as "any repeated pattern of behavior, or perception of behavior, that interferes with or is at risk of interfering with optimal learning or engagement in prosocial interactions with peers and adults" (Smith & Fox 2003, 6). Challenging behavior can signal difficulty with social and emotional adjustment—foundational competencies that are linked to children's school readiness and later school success (Fantuzzo et al. 2007).

Although challenging behavior can occur in any classroom, research indicates that some children in urban communities experience conditions that contribute to risk factors for social and emotional delays (Fox, Dunlap, & Powell 2002). In addition, there is a specific need to support children who live in poverty, as children in poor families are twice as likely to be at risk for developmental, behavioral, and social delays as children in families earning 200 percent or more of the federal poverty line (Children's Defense Fund 2014). That is, while 10 to 21 percent of all preschool children show challenging behavior such as aggression, noncompliance, defiance, tantrums, and property destruction, 30 percent of children who live in poverty exhibit such behaviors (Voorhees et al. 2013).

In this article, we describe five culturally responsive core strategies to promote positive teacher relationships with young children in preschool and minimize challenging behavior: learn about children and families, develop and teach expectations, take the child's perspective, teach and model empathy, and use group times to discuss conflict. As African American boys experience a much higher rate of suspensions and expulsions from preschool settings than do other children (Gilliam 2005), these relationship-building techniques are particularly relevant for teachers as they reflect on their own practices and biases—especially toward African American boys—in early childhood classrooms.

Learn About Children and Families

A core consideration in developmentally appropriate practice and cultural responsiveness is that practitioners learn about each child and family and intentionally adapt and respond to each child's strengths and needs (Derman-Sparks & Edwards with Goins 2020; NAEYC 2022). Culturally responsive practice is often defined as using the experiences and perspectives of children and their families as a tool to support them more effectively (Gay 2002). As this approach is child and family centered, it sets the stage for critical relationship building (Ford & Kea 2009).

Teachers can partner with families by inviting them to visit the classroom and participate in activities with their child. Teachers can also arrange to visit children at home, where they may engage in informal discussions with family members about what children enjoy doing for fun and learn about their favorite food, toy, or song. These interactions can reveal cultural values and norms in the home environment. Families may also share information about their child's temperament, primary play partners, and home language (NAEYC 1995). Meetings at school with families might address family routines, religious holidays and traditions, and activities the families enjoy in the community. Teachers can use information they learn about a child and family to support the child's social and emotional adjustment to the early childhood environment. Further, these conversations can demonstrate that not all children and families within a particular racial or ethnic group display similar characteristics, which is a potential teacher bias (Ford & Kea 2009). Sharing a short, warm anecdote with families, in person or in a note, about something their child did that day assures parents that the teacher cares about their child and makes an effort to know the child individually. This further connects families to their child's classroom community.

During a recent conversation with Miles's mother, Mrs. Green learned that Miles's father is a musician and that Miles really enjoys music. Miles's mother explained that Miles likes to dance and sing to his favorite songs, moving vigorously around the house. Mrs. Green used her knowledge about Miles's interest to plan music and movement activities for future morning circles to engage Miles.

Develop and Teach Expectations

The second culturally responsive strategy in the pyramid model framework is developing and teaching two to five classroom expectations that are linked to the values and cultures of the children, teachers, and families. Expectations should be positively stated and developmentally appropriate and should apply to both children and adults (teachers and families) (Steed & Pomerleau 2012). After cultivating a better understanding of children and families, early childhood teachers can base expectations on shared values and connections to cultures. Young children should be included in forming guidelines for behavior, as they are more likely to understand and follow them when they have input. Examples of expectations for preschool children include "Be a Friend, Be Safe, and Be a Helper" and "Use Listening Ears, Use Gentle Touches, and Use Walking Feet."

Expectations need to be consistently emphasized to prevent challenging behavior. In addition to responding to opportunities that arise during the day, teachers decide how and when they will teach, model, and positively reinforce the expectations across environments (circle time, music and movement activities, recess, lunch/snack) so that the guidelines and associated behaviors become part of the program culture (Benedict, Horner, & Squires 2007). Many teachers develop songs and hand movements to go with their expectations. Other approaches include modeling, using puppets, reading stories, and role-playing. Pictures of the children, teachers, and staff demonstrating the expectations can be posted in classrooms and common areas for further encouragement.

Pyramid Model Framework

The five core strategies we suggest are informed by fundamental principles of the pyramid model (Fox & Hemmeter 2009)—a comprehensive framework for addressing the social and emotional outcomes of young children (Hemmeter, Ostrosky, & Fox 2006). The pyramid model includes three levels of support: universal prevention strategies for use with all children; secondary social and emotional approaches for children at risk for social and emotional delays; and tertiary individualized and function-based interventions for children with persistent challenges (Fox & Hemmeter 2009).

To reinforce positive behavior and to bring the actions to children's attention, it is important to verbally acknowledge children and adults when they demonstrate expectations. When a child's behavior reflects a great example of an expectation such as "Be a Friend"—like helping another child clean up a spill at lunch or inviting a new child to build a block tower—teachers can write a note of thanks or give the child an opportunity to wear a "Super Friend" cape. A bulletin board in a common area provides a public place to post notecards recognizing adults who demonstrate examples of meeting program expectations ("Miss Wilma was a helper today when she fixed Erin's hearing device!").

To be culturally responsive, it is important that expectations reflect the values and cultures of families and teachers and other staff in the school. For example, in cultures that value community over independence (Ford & Kea 2009), guidelines for some activities (like snack) may emphasize relationship-building behaviors—passing the food bowl—over independent adaptive skills—taking an appropriate portion of a self-serve snack.

Develop and Teach Empathy

Another culturally responsive strategy for supporting positive relationships is empathy—concern for others arising from an emotional connection. Empathetic individuals apply interpersonal sensitivity to understand the experiences of others in order to provide support or assistance (Berliner & Masterson 2015). Researchers have long theorized that empathy is a critical component in teacher effectiveness in urban settings, positively impacting teachers' dispositions in interactions with students of color (Warren 2014). Thus, it is important for teachers in urban settings to model and encourage empathy to foster a culturally responsive classroom environment.

To develop and teach empathy, teachers first have to know themselves (Derman-Sparks & Edwards with Goins 2020). It is necessary for teachers to engage in critical self-reflection to uncover implicit personal biases and assumptions, and bridge understanding across cultural groups (Cooper, He, & Levin 2011; Price 2015). Whether subconscious or explicit, teachers' negative perceptions about children who differ from them in terms of culture, race, or ethnic identity can impact the teachers' ability to teach effectively and create empathetic classrooms.

Teachers can help children learn empathetic behavior by modeling warm and responsive actions, like anticipating and responding promptly to children's needs and worries, and greeting children with a smile (Twardosz 2005). Using storybooks, games, and music is another way to teach empathy. Teachers can create lessons and activities that highlight respect, kindness, compassion, and responsibility—and help children discover similarities with peers from different backgrounds (Berliner & Masterson 2015). Teachers can ponder reflective questions, such as, *What are my initial reactions to this child and their family?, What do my reactions tell me about my personal beliefs and assumptions?,* and *What can I do to build the child's and family's trust?* (Collins, Arthur, & Wong-Wylie 2010; Price 2015). Although there is work to be done to unpack the contextual factors that may explain why African American boys are expelled and suspended at a higher rate than other preschool children, self-reflective questions like these and those offered throughout *Anti-Bias Education for Young Children and Ourselves* (Derman-Sparks & Edwards with Goins 2020) are one place to start.

Historically, picture books have featured mostly White characters (Larrick 1965). When choosing high-quality books for the classroom, make sure that the characters reflect the ethnic makeup of your classroom (Koss 2014; Larrick 1965), as it is important for all children, and particularly those of color, to "see themselves" in books. During these lessons, teachers can teach relevant emotion vocabulary (Joseph, Strain, & Ostrosky 2008), read books, and sing songs that reflect the children's cultures. According to the tenets of Afrocentric teaching—which harnesses the skills African American children bring to schools to engage them in the classroom experience (Ford & Kea 2009)—combining music with creative movement, mime, and dance is a form of expression for many African American children and engages them in shared affective experiences that are useful for empathy development (Boykin 1994; Laird 2015).

> ## Additional Resources
>
> › National Center for Pyramid Model Innovations (NCPMI)—www.challengingbehavior.org
> › Pyramid Model Consortium—www.pyramidmodel.org

For example, in a jubilant rendition, Miles and Carmen share a toy drum and a tambourine as they dance to a popular song heard in their communities. The song promotes unity, friendship, and love. Through group music making, children can express feelings and connect with the feelings of others, promoting positive social and emotional development.

Perspective Taking

A fourth culturally responsive strategy, perspective taking, has been defined as the capacity to understand another's thoughts, feelings, or internal states (DeBernardis, Hayes, & Fryling 2014). Through the use of affective statements, teachers can reframe a child's challenging behavior and focus on the child's internal state. Affective statements are "I" statements that express a feeling, precisely describe a child's behavior, and make the child aware of the positive or negative impact of the behavior (Costello, Wachtel, & Wachtel 2009). Take, for example, a child who often transitions from lunch to outdoor time by pushing their way through classmates to discard their trash and dash to the playground door. A teacher might say, "Stop running in the classroom. When you run in the classroom, our friends are not safe." To reframe the child's behavior, the teacher might consider that the child is excited to play outside. From this perspective, the teacher could rephrase their statement: "I see that you are really excited about going outside. Thank you for putting your dish in the trash, but please remember to use your walking feet and move around your friends." When teachers use affective statements to reframe a child's challenging behavior, it demonstrates their understanding of the child's perspective. Miles's teacher used an affective statement that considered his perspective about morning circle when she stated, "Miles, I see that you are upset because you do not want to sit at morning circle and want to play with the musical instruments instead."

Using Group Time to Discuss Conflict

The final culturally responsive strategy drawing from the pyramid model framework is using group time to resolve conflict. This allows for a restorative justice approach, which offers those involved in the conflict an opportunity for reconciliation. Although many children benefit from the use of group time to address conflict and this approach can promote inclusion, as opposed to exclusion (e.g., time out), as a response to challenging behavior, it is important to develop methods and awareness so children do not feel shamed during the process but rather part of a trusting community of problem solvers. When done well, problem solving as a group can foster active engagement and learning and enable children and adults to build strong relationships. The teacher can establish the tone for the group by reading a poem about friendship or sharing a culturally relevant and familiar quote from a song, movie, or book. Next, it is helpful to remind children of the expectations for the discussion: "We've been practicing how to listen and how to talk at group time. Let's remember to wait calmly for our turn to speak, make eye contact with the person to whom we're talking, and use kind words." In some cases, teachers can minimize challenging behavior by conducting group time prior to situations with potential for challenging behavior (before a field trip, in the beginning of the school year, prior to implementing a change to the environment) (Costello, Wachtel, & Wachtel 2009; Pautz 2009).

Conclusion

Young children with challenging behavior are often rejected by their peers and receive less positive feedback from teachers than their peers do (Hemmeter, Ostrosky, & Fox 2006). Early childhood classrooms are a primary setting for teaching skills that are critical for young children's social and emotional development. Given the large amount of time many children spend in these settings, it is important that strong, positive teacher-child relationships be nurtured to ensure that children receive the support needed to promote positive social and emotional development (Bronfenbrenner 1977) and school readiness in general (Williford et al. 2013). Practitioners in urban settings play a valuable role in young children's social and emotional development by providing supports that are relevant and appropriate.

The five culturally responsive strategies described in this article can guide teachers in creating a classroom atmosphere that not only responds to children's challenging behavior but also anticipates their needs. Implementation of these strategies helps teachers initiate sustainable relationships and nurturing classrooms where all children are valued and have opportunities to grow and develop. The more children get together and engage in prosocial interactions with teachers and peers, the happier everyone will truly be.

Reflection Questions

1. How does your perspective influence how you talk and interact with the family members of children who have a different culture, race, ethnicity, and/or ability than yours?

2. Think about your initial reactions when you meet a child whose culture, race, ethnicity, and/or ability is different from your own. Do you have any assumptions about the child that are different than the assumptions you have about a child who shares an identity similar to your own? Do you assume that a child with a different culture, race, ethnicity, and/or ability is capable of success in your classroom? How do your assumptions impact how you might perceive and respond to children's varying levels of social competence?

3. As you reflect on the ways you perceive and react to cultural, racial, ethnic, and/or ability differences, what have you learned about your personal beliefs and assumptions? How might you take action to address your assumptions and ensure you provide a supportive approach to all children?

REFERENCES

Benedict, E.A., R.H. Horner, & J.K. Squires. 2007. "Assessment and Implementation of Positive Behavior Support in Preschools." *Topics in Early Childhood Special Education* 27 (3): 174–92.

Berliner, R., & T.L. Masterson. 2015. "Review of the Research: Promoting Empathy Development in the Early Childhood and Elementary Classroom." *Childhood Education* 91 (1): 57–64.

Boykin, A.W. 1994. "Afrocultural Expression and Its Implications for Schooling." In *Teaching Diverse Populations: Formulating a Knowledge Base*, eds. E.R. Hollins, J.E. King, & W.C. Hayman, 243–56. Albany: State University of New York Press.

Bronfenbrenner, U. 1977. "Toward an Experimental Ecology of Human Development." *American Psychologist* 32 (7): 515–31.

Children's Defense Fund. 2014. *The State of America's Children*. Washington, DC: Children's Defense Fund. www.childrensdefense.org/wp-content/uploads/2023/08/2014-soac.pdf.

Collins, S., N. Arthur, & G. Wong-Wylie. 2010. "Enhancing Reflective Practice in Multicultural Counseling Through Cultural Auditing." *Journal of Counseling and Development* 88 (3): 340–47.

Cooper, J.E., Y. He, & B.B. Levin. 2011. *Developing Critical Cultural Competence: A Guide for 21st Century Educators*. Thousand Oaks, CA: Sage.

Costello, B., J. Wachtel, & T. Wachtel. 2009. *The Restorative Practices Handbook for Teachers, Disciplinarians, and Administrators*. Bethlehem, PA: International Institute for Restorative Practices.

DeBernardis, G.M., L.J. Hayes, & M.J. Fryling. 2014. "Perspective Taking as a Continuum." *Psychological Record* 64 (1): 123–31.

Derman-Sparks, L., & J.O. Edwards. With C. Goins. 2020. *Anti-Bias Education for Young Children and Ourselves*. 2nd ed. Washington, DC: NAEYC.

Fantuzzo, J., R. Bulotsky-Shearer, P. McDermott, C. McWayne, D. Frye, & S. Perlman. 2007. "Investigation of Dimensions of Social-Emotional Classroom Behavior and School Readiness for Low-Income Urban Preschool Children." *School Psychology Review* 36 (1): 44–62.

Ford, D.Y., & C.D. Kea. 2009. "Creating Culturally Responsive Instruction: For Students' and Teachers' Sakes." *Focus on Exceptional Children* 41 (9): 1–16.

Fox, L., G. Dunlap, & D. Powell. 2002. "Young Children with Challenging Behavior: Issues and Considerations for Behavior Support." *Journal of Positive Behavior Interventions* 4 (4): 208–17.

Fox, L., & M.L. Hemmeter. 2009. "A Program-Wide Model for Supporting Social Emotional Development and Addressing Challenging Behavior in Early Childhood Settings." In *Handbook of Positive Behavior Support*, eds. W. Sailor, G. Dunlap, G. Sugai, & R. Horner, 177–202. New York: Springer.

Gay, G. 2002. "Preparing for Culturally Responsive Teaching." *Journal of Teacher Education* 53 (2): 106–16.

Gilliam, W.S. 2005. *Prekindergartners Left Behind: Expulsion Rates in the State in Prekindergarten Programs*. New Haven, CT: Yale University Child Study Center.

Hemmeter, M.L., M.M. Ostrosky, & L. Fox. 2006. "Social and Emotional Foundations for Early Learning: A Conceptual Model for Intervention." *School Psychology Review* 35 (4): 583–601.

Joseph, G., P. Strain, & M.M. Ostrosky. 2008. *Fostering Emotional Literacy in Young Children: Labeling Emotions*. What Works Brief #21. Champaign, IL: Center on the Social and Emotional Foundations of Learning. http://csefel.vanderbilt.edu/kits/wwbtk21.pdf.

Koss, M. 2014. "Diversity in Contemporary Picture Books: A Content Analysis." *Journal of Children's Literature* 41 (1): 32–42.

Laird, L. 2015. "Empathy in the Classroom: Can Music Bring Us More in Tune With One Another?" *Music Educators Journal* 101 (4): 56–61.

Larrick, N. 1965. "The All-White World of Children's Books." *Saturday Review* (1): 63–65.

NAEYC. 1995. "Responding to Linguistic and Cultural Diversity. Recommendations for Effective Early Childhood Education." Position statement. Washington, DC: NAEYC. www.naeyc.org/files/naeyc/file/positions/PSDIV98.PDF.

NAEYC. 2022. *Developmentally Appropriate Practice in Early Childhood Programs Serving Children from Birth Through Age 8*. 4th ed. Washington, DC: NAEYC.

Pautz, M.-I. 2009. "Empowering the Next Generation: Restorative Practices in a Preschool." *Restorative Practices EForum*. www.iirp.edu/news/empowering-the-next-generation-restorative-practices-in-a-preschool.

Price, C. 2015. "Reflective Questions for Early Interventionists and Early Childhood Special Educators." Presentation at the Annual International Conference of the Division for Early Childhood of the Council for Exceptional Children, in Atlanta, Georgia.

Smith, B., & L. Fox. 2003. *Systems of Service Delivery: A Synthesis of Evidence Relevant to Young Children at Risk of or Who Have Challenging Behavior*. Tampa, FL: Center for Evidence-Based Practice: Young Children with Challenging Behavior.

Steed, E.A., & T. Pomerleau. 2012. *Preschool-Wide Evaluation Tool (PreSet) Manual, Research Edition: Assessing Universal Program-Wide Positive Behavior Support in Early Childhood*. Baltimore: Brookes.

Twardosz, S. 2005. *Expressing Warmth and Affection to Children*. What Works Brief #20. Nashville: Center on the Social and Emotional Foundations for Early Learning. http://csefel.vanderbilt.edu/briefs/wwb20.pdf.

Voorhees, M.D., L.V. Walker, M.E. Snell, & C.G. Smith. 2013. "A Demonstration of Individualized Positive Behavior Support Interventions by Head Start Staff to Address Children's Challenging Behavior." *Research and Practice for Persons with Severe Disabilities* 38 (3): 173–85.

Warren, C.A. 2014. "Towards a Pedagogy for the Application of Empathy in Culturally Diverse Classrooms." *Urban Review* 46 (3): 395–419.

Williford, A.P., M.F. Maier, J.T. Downer, R.C. Pianta, & C. Howes. 2013. "Understanding How Children's Engagement and Teachers' Interactions Combine to Predict School Readiness." *Journal of Applied Developmental Psychology* 34 (6): 299–309.

About the Authors

Charis L. Wahman, PhD, BCBA-D, is assistant professor of special education at Michigan State University. She also serves as a clinician in early care settings to support young children with social and emotional needs. Charis has conducted research, published articles, and presented on the social and emotional development of young children and families' experiences with suspension and expulsion at national conferences.

Elizabeth A. Steed, PhD, is professor in the early childhood education program at the University of Colorado Denver. She has conducted research, published articles, presented at conferences, and served on state leadership teams focused on improving the social and emotional competence of young children.

Culturally Appropriate Positive Guidance with Young Children

Zeynep Isik-Ercan

Three-year-old Triston is singing to a rag doll in the dramatic play area, pretending to rock her to sleep. Ana, also 3, snatches the doll from Triston's hands. Ana says, "Baby wants sleep!" Upset, Triston says, "It's my baby! I am rocking her to sleep!" Ana insists that the baby needs to be under the blanket. She lies down with the doll for a second, then jumps up to close the blinds.

At first glance, a teacher may view this situation as a behavioral issue—Ana needs to understand that no one can take another's toy without permission. While the behavior is important to address, Ana and Triston's teacher, Ms. Jones, is also aware that young children have a deep understanding of their own cultural routines and a strong desire to follow those routines. While acknowledging that Ana's method was not appropriate, Ms. Jones realizes that Ana was trying to prevent an uncomfortable situation for the "baby" by putting her to sleep according to the routine in Ana's home—lying down with the baby in a quiet, dark room.

To help all of her students understand that everyone has different cultural practices at home, and that all of them are to be respected, Ms. Jones decides to begin an exploration of the different ways children and families go to sleep. She searches for children's literature focused on how people go to sleep and chooses *Where Children Sleep,* by James Mollison; *Why Cowboys Sleep with Their Boots On,* by Laurie Knowlton, illustrated by James Rice; and *The Napping House,* by Audrey Wood, illustrated by Don Wood. As Ms. Jones reads these books aloud, she supports the children in exploring the illustrations and comparing their home routines with those in the books. To broaden the discussions, Ms. Jones shows them photographs she found online that depict the bedtime rituals of children from various countries. Many of these photos show how weather, house size and type, and parenting practices influence the ways children go to sleep. Within a few days, Ms. Jones and the children carry the investigation into the dramatic play area, where they pretend to put babies to sleep in hammocks, body wraps, cribs, beds, and sleeping bags, either alone or with dolls representing parents or siblings.

Although it is not possible to transform every incident into an enriching investigation, teachers of children ages 2 to 6 would do well to follow in Ms. Jones's footsteps. Many behaviors have cultural roots that teachers can capitalize on to foster each child's developing identity, share cultural lessons with the whole class, and help children cultivate shared norms for their behavior as students. Research on the experiences of culturally and linguistically diverse young children in early childhood settings implies that what Ms. Jones faced is fairly common: some guidance challenges are based on differences between home and school practices (Rogoff 2003). Teachers like Ms. Jones recognize that some conflicts among children reflect the children's early understanding of their own cultural scripts (family and community practices and rituals for how things are done) and their limited understanding of others' scripts.

As teachers provide positive, developmentally appropriate guidance for a particular behavior, they consider the issue through the lens of *cultural appropriateness,* an important dimension of developmentally appropriate practice (NAEYC 2022). This lens may encompass family traditions, religious beliefs, community etiquette, social class, and contextual differences (such as urban, rural, and suburban practices), any of which may be a source of possible conflict between children. As they choose guidance strategies, teachers help children understand that

their peers' play and behavior may look and feel different from their own because of different cultural practices, and they support children as they gradually learn to negotiate different sets of expectations between home and early education settings.

Early childhood educators may find that the expectations of some children and families they serve do not fit their framework for positive guidance. Culturally appropriate positive guidance requires educators to understand and mediate differing views on child guidance between home and school contexts.

Understanding Family Perspectives and Goals for Child Development

One important aspect of child development is children's increasing adoption of and participation in family and community routines and practices (Rogoff 2003). Some cultural practices, such as authoritarian parenting styles, may seem to conflict with an education program's philosophy and curriculum or with a practitioner's own perspective. (See "Understanding Family Practices that Clash with Center Principles" on page 29) However, by respecting families' viewpoints and contexts, practitioners support family cohesion, which is an essential aspect of social and emotional development in young children, especially children whose home culture might be very different from the typical US school culture (Isik-Ercan 2012).

Young children benefit when teachers and families establish healthy partnerships and define common goals or developmental outcomes for children. When early childhood practitioners inquire about particular family practices, they are likely to find that both parties have many similar goals, including helping children develop skills such as social competency, altruism, sharing, collaboration, respect, and confidence (Isik-Ercan 2010). While these goals look similar across cultural contexts, the tools and methods each party uses for positive guidance might look quite different. Therefore, practitioners may need to engage with families in collaborative problem solving when conflicts arise (NAEYC 2022), rather than apply one guidance method for all children. The following example illustrates how Mr. Garcia, a preschool teacher, used culturally appropriate guidance.

> When 5-year-old Yen-Ting sees 4-year-old Max playing with his cereal and dropping it on the floor, Yen-Ting quietly says, "Shame on you." Max shouts, "Go away!"
>
> Yen-Ting is upset by Max's reaction. He was reminding Max about the no-playing-with-food rule, like an older brother might. Max, offended by the intrusion into his privacy, thinks Yen-Ting should not reprimand him, as he is not an authority figure. This exchange reveals the differences in the cultural perspectives these children have gained in their family contexts.
>
> Mr. Garcia is knowledgeable about both families' expectations for their children. For example, from conversations with Yen-Ting's family, he knows that saving face to avoid public shame and preserve group harmony is an important Confucian principle. Instead of bringing both children together to address the issue—a common conflict resolution technique—Mr. Garcia discreetly speaks individually to the children to help each understand the other's perspective. He explains to Max that Yen-Ting is trying to be considerate by quietly reminding him of a rule; he tells Yen-Ting that even though he was whispering, his words sounded harsh to Max. Mr. Garcia suggests that in the future, Max consider whether his classmates are trying to help him, and Yen-Ting consider saying, "If you drop food on the floor, the floor will be dirty and wet," and let Max make the choice. Although the boys did not engage in conflict resolution in this instance, they are now more aware of each other's intentions.

When they use culturally appropriate positive guidance, practitioners like Mr. Garcia support the development of children's bicultural identities, honoring both their family and community context and their school context. Some home practices are directly associated with the core of children's cultural identity and so should be respected. By respecting such practices—even when not agreeing with them—educators promote children's healthy social and emotional growth. In offering guidance, Mr. Garcia protected the families' position as primary caregivers and guides in their children's social and emotional growth, as suggested in the NAEYC "Code of Ethical Conduct" ([2005] 2011), in particular, Ideal I-2.6—"To acknowledge families' childrearing values and their right to make decisions for their children."

Understanding Family Practices that Clash with Center Principles

Some family practices may pose guidance challenges in early learning programs.

Family cultural practice	Center principle	Interpretation of a family practice
› Spoon-feeding toddlers while sharing stories and songs with them (not allowing young toddlers to practice self-feeding) › Performing physical care tasks and practices for children, such as tying their shoes or putting their coats on them	› Encouraging young children's self-care practices and self-help skills to foster independence	› Spilling and wasting food is unacceptable and disrespectful of people's efforts/nature's bounty/animals in the food chain. › Feeding rituals and other physical care customs are essential elements in establishing physical and emotional attachment between caregiver and child and are shared cultural rituals that signify love.

Using Sociocultural Conflicts Among Children as Teachable Moments: A Case Study

Guidance challenges stemming from cultural and linguistic diversity can be viewed as opportunities for practitioners to address children's growing social abilities. An early childhood practitioner can help culturally diverse children understand norms and social expectations by mediating peer relationships. The following story illustrates such a process.

Four-year-old Abdi was a newly arrived refugee from Somalia. On his first day at a church-located early childhood center, he ran wildly down a hallway, followed by his mother, who was attempting to stop him. Teachers were startled to see a child making so much noise and running freely in the orderly and quiet learning environment. Interacting with Abdi in the following days, Ms. Miller, the preschool preservice teacher, and I learned that he was extremely nervous in his new, all-White preschool class and wanted to leave, so running seemed to him like a good solution.

By the following week, however, Abdi was settling in, following directions and seeming more at ease with his peers. Ms. Miller and I often observed Abdi gently touching his friends on their shoulders and heads while participating in whole group games and engaging in rough-and-tumble play on the playground—sometimes to his peers' dismay. Ms. Miller and I worked with Abdi and his peers to explore social expectations in his new environment.

For example, Abdi's peers had a much larger sphere of personal space than Abdi was accustomed to, so he would often talk more closely or touch more often than they preferred. Although his peers protected each other's personal space, they could not explain to Abdi how or why they felt he was violating it.

Being careful to not put Abdi on the spot, Ms. Miller and I facilitated this negotiation of personal space by helping all the children understand some expectations in our early childhood classroom. We discussed and role-played rules about private space, noise-level expectations, and limited physical contact. Using persona dolls in story lines that children developed and explored, we guided the children's discussion of why, how, and when touching friends may or may not be a good idea in the school setting and other settings. Like Ms. Jones's investigation of sleeping routines, we explored the notion of personal space as a fascinating cultural difference—not as something that could be right or wrong.

We also helped children understand that some nonverbal clues, such as smiling or making eye contact, may, in certain contexts, mean discomfort rather than agreement or contentment. These practices provided children with tools to notice subtle cues before unwelcome interactions turned into negative reactions.

At the same time, in collaboration with the classroom teacher, Ms. Miller and I helped the individual children who were most reactive to Abdi realize that when Abdi kept touching a child, it meant he was showing his affection for and interest in that child. Discussing differences in children's actions supported all children's general perspective-taking abilities. In the next week, we observed several children explaining to each other what a peer meant when they said or did something that might be misunderstood.

Making a Program's Structure More Accommodating

Another way to encompass varying perspectives on child guidance is to provide a flexible program structure that accommodates individual needs. For instance, children who come from homes where their schedules flow with the natural rhythms of their attention span and engagement and with their own awareness of their physical needs might struggle in a more structured classroom environment.

Simple arrangements such as making a snack available at a corner table, where children can sit whenever they need a break, might offer a natural respite and sense of control for children who might be frustrated with and resistant to what they perceive as unnatural transitions and abrupt changes.

Children's Flexibility and Resilience in Negotiating Multiple Learning Contexts

When it comes to forming bicultural identities, children are remarkably adaptive. For example, a case study of a preschool classroom found that although teachers and parents of culturally diverse children held different beliefs and practices about literacy learning, appropriate language for interactions, and social norms, the children were successful in navigating both the home and classroom contexts (Fluckiger 2010). They used strategies such as following the peer culture rules they observed when entering ongoing play or showing their knowledge of the alphabet, so that other children sought out their knowledge and showed greater acceptance of them. Most young children become skilled at analyzing the cultural codes and expectations in the classroom (Kim 2014); in fact, growing research evidence suggests that children's understanding of others affects their behavior in positive ways, leading to greater acceptance by peers (Spinrad & VanSchyndel 2015). Rather than anticipate sociocultural conflict among children when cultural incongruences arise, teachers can observe and build on children's established and emerging abilities to adjust to different contexts.

Understanding Peer Culture and Fostering Classroom Community

Peer culture—"the stable sets of routines, artifacts, values, and concerns that children produce and share with each other" (Corsaro 2012, 489)—is an important component of classroom culture. Teachers may gain valuable insights when they examine various elements of the peer culture in their classrooms and use children's interactions to establish positive guidance. One study (personal communication with Elena Bodrova, April 30, 2013) noted that when provided with autonomy to do so, preschool children first monitor and regulate their peers' behavior before they turn to themselves and apply the same strategies, aligning with Vygotsky's (1978) statement that mental skills begin as social processes and then become internalized. Social interaction with peers during play provides children with necessary feedback to reconsider their actions. Even though their home practices might be different, Chen (2012) documented children's flexibility to use feedback gathered from those peer interactions. For example, a child might ask a group of children several times to play with them and routinely be told no. Over time, the child may observe that incorporating a toy or adding a prop or character to the play without directly asking for permission may work better (Van Hoorn et al. 2014). Creating a safe space in which children can monitor each other and thus better internalize guidance expectations helps foster a close-knit classroom community.

When practitioners attend to the peer culture in their classrooms, they may notice that children are curious to explore their peers' beliefs and behavioral norms, which at times might lead to what may seem like discriminatory behavior (Derman-Sparks & Edwards with Goins 2020) and—when not addressed—to guidance challenges. For example, when Susan, who was new to preschool, shouted to her peers, "No boys allowed in our kitchen!," she was drawing on roles she was familiar with—a homemaker woman and a breadwinner man. Having gotten to know Susan, her teacher saw that she was thinking through these roles and wanted to provoke the boys to see if they agreed with them. When practitioners understand children's curiosity and the challenge of digesting multiple viewpoints, they may be encouraged to provide space for children to explore differences and variations in social or individual practices through dramatic play, instead of viewing differences as offending and limiting this crucial time for children to negotiate their actions and beliefs.

Reflection Questions

1. In what contexts or situations in the classroom might you be likely to observe cultural conflicts among children? How could you use these as teachable moments?

2. What are some routines you could incorporate into your day to support children's growing understanding of diverse practices?

3. How can you model a classroom culture of inclusion and belonging? Think of one strategy you may already have in place and one new strategy to use.

4. Consider the ways each of the children and families you serve and their cultural practices are reflected in the classroom. What are some cultural practices tied to daily life and life experiences that are shared or different among your class?

Conclusion

For many children, preschool is their first significant opportunity to learn about routines and behaviors that are different from their home life. Keep in mind that differences in cultural routines can be just as hard—if not harder—to adjust to as differences in when and where children are eating and napping. To examine their cultural assumptions, educators should challenge themselves by taking another colleague's or a family's perspective on child guidance (Gonzalez-Mena 2010). Agreement may not always be possible, but understanding and respect can always grow. As practitioners develop their cultural knowledge, they will be better able to identify opportunities for learning, just as Ms. Jones and Mr. Garcia did.

REFERENCES

Chen, X. 2012. "Culture, Peer Interaction, and Socioemotional Development." *Child Development Perspectives* 6 (1): 27–34.

Corsaro, W.A. 2012. "Interpretive Reproduction in Children's Play." *American Journal of Play* 4 (4): 488–504.

Derman-Sparks, L., & J.O. Edwards. With C. Goins. 2020. *Anti-Bias Education for Young Children and Ourselves.* 2nd ed. Washington, DC: NAEYC.

Fluckiger, B. 2010. "Culture-Switching in Different Worlds: Young Children's Transition Experiences." *Australasian Journal of Early Childhood* 35 (4): 101–08.

Gonzalez-Mena, J. 2010. "Cultural Responsiveness and Routines: When Center and Home Don't Match." *Exchange* 194: 42–44.

Isik-Ercan, Z. 2010. "Looking at School from the House Window: Learning from Turkish-American Parents' Experiences with Early Elementary Education in the United States." *Early Childhood Education Journal* 38 (2): 133–42.

Isik-Ercan, Z. 2012. "In Pursuit of a New Perspective in the Education of Children of the Refugees: Advocacy for the 'Family.'" *Educational Sciences: Theory and Practice* 12 (4): 3025–38.

Kim, J. 2014. "'You Don't Need to Be Mean. We're Friends, Right?' Young Korean-American Children's Conflicts and References to Friendship." *Journal of Early Childhood Research* 12 (3): 279–93.

NAEYC. (2005) 2011. "Code of Ethical Conduct and Statement of Commitment." Position statement. Washington, DC: NAEYC. www.naeyc.org/resources/position-statements/ethical-conduct.

NAEYC. 2022. *Developmentally Appropriate Practice in Early Childhood Programs Serving Children from Birth Through Age 8.* 4th ed. Washington, DC: NAEYC.

Rogoff, B. 2003. *The Cultural Nature of Human Development.* New York: Oxford University Press.

Spinrad, T.L., & S. VanSchyndel. 2015. "Socio-Cognitive Correlates of Prosocial Behaviour in Young Children." In *Encyclopedia on Early Childhood Development* [online], eds. R.E. Tremblay, M. Boivin, & R.D. Peters, topic ed. A. Knafo-Noam. www.child-encyclopedia.com/prosocial-behaviour/according-experts/socio-cognitive-correlates-prosocial-behaviour-young-children.

Van Hoorn, J., P.M. Nourot, B. Scales, & K.R. Alward. 2014. *Play at the Center of the Curriculum.* 6th ed. Upper Saddle River, NJ: Pearson.

Vygotsky, L.S. 1978. *Mind in Society: The Development of Higher Psychological Processes.* Cambridge, MA: Harvard University Press.

About the Author

Zeynep Isik-Ercan, PhD, is professor of education and department chair of early childhood, elementary education, and critical foundation at Rowan University. She is also codirector of the Early Childhood Leadership Institute, a professional development and research institute. Zeynep leads research, training, and evaluation projects; writes for academic journals; and teaches and speaks on a variety of topics, including best practices for cultural and linguistic diversity, intellectual development, and professional development of educators and leaders.

Understanding Young Children's Play

Seeing Behavior Through the Lens of Attachment Theory

Shulamit N. Ritblatt and Sascha Longstreth

Preschool teachers play a major role in providing young children with the secure attachment base and sense of safety that are needed for healthy development (Hamre & Pianta 2001). By modeling and genuinely engaging in warm, caring interactions every day, they help young children learn to construct healthy templates for current and future relationships. These positive interactions are especially critical for children who have challenging behavior (Silver et al. 2005). While children with challenging behavior can leave teachers feeling frustrated and helpless (Spilt & Koomen 2009), we need to remember that they are among the children who need us the most!

Because play is a primary means for children to interact with others (Piaget & Inhelder 1962), carefully observing children's interactions during play is an excellent vehicle for adults to understand children in the context of relationships. By intentionally watching and reflecting on children's play behaviors, preschool teachers can better understand the different ways young children perceive people and the environment as either safe and trustworthy, or not. To help teachers broaden their meaning-making process when encountering various play behaviors, it can be helpful to consider behavior through the lens of attachment theory. Although teachers should avoid categorizing children by attachment style (because determining attachment requires specialized training and assessments), considering attachment as one of several factors can assist teachers in providing sensitive care to children.

What Is Attachment?

Attachment is a deep and sustained emotional bond between an individual and an attachment figure, usually a caregiver (Bowlby [1969] 1983). Psychologists have identified three attachment patterns: secure, insecure-avoidant, and insecure-ambivalent (Ainsworth et al. 1978). While children who have a secure attachment pattern tend to assess new situations accurately and explore situations with confidence, children who display either of the two insecure attachment patterns tend to have difficulty distinguishing between situations that are safe and those that are threatening (Wismer Fries et al. 2005). They may exhibit anxious behaviors in neutral circumstances that they misperceive as threatening (Schore 2001). This anxiety may reduce exploration, leading to children showing less interest in play materials, less maturity in their play with objects, and a lower likelihood of initiating social play with peers (Ainsworth et al. 1978; McElwain & Volling 2004).

Although the attachment types are distinct, children's behavior is often ambiguous because so many different factors influence behavior (e.g., crankiness can occur when a child doesn't get enough sleep, is hungry, or wants more attention). The following vignettes, all snapshots from one classroom, illustrate the three attachment patterns and how they might be reflected in children's play behaviors. Use the attachment lens to deepen your understanding, but keep in mind that there are multiple complex underlying factors that can account for differences in the play behaviors of these—and all—children.

Vignettes by Attachment Patterns

Secure

Marissa, 49 months old, has been busy much of the morning building a block city that includes a school, a hospital, and several houses. As she begins construction on the roads, Alex asks her what she is building. She tells him that she is making a city and asks if he would like to help. He kneels down and begins constructing an airport.

After a couple of minutes, Alex states that he does not have any more rectangle blocks, which he needs to create runways. Marissa looks around and finds another block shape that she thinks will work. "Here, try this one," she tells him. Alex looks doubtful but tries her suggestion, and to his surprise, it works! They continue to play together until it is time for lunch.

When young children experience secure, stable attachment relationships with their primary caregivers, they are more likely to develop self-confidence, motivation to learn, and the courage to explore their physical world (Sroufe 2005; Thompson 2008). Marissa demonstrates how a secure child might

engage in play in an early childhood setting. Marissa freely explores the materials, working purposefully with pleasure. She interacts with her peers calmly and positively (Behrens, Hesse, & Main 2007). She is capable of working with a peer toward a common play goal (building an airport) and of activating key friendship skills (e.g., sharing, initiating ideas).

Not surprisingly, securely attached children are more likely to be socially competent throughout childhood than children who are insecurely attached (Raby et al. 2015) and more likely to have higher-quality friendships characterized by more harmony, intimacy, and empathy (McElwain & Volling 2004). When a problem arises, Marissa is usually able to regulate her frustration and problem solve by trying alternative solutions. Should her frustration rise to a level of distress, Marissa would readily go to her caregiver for soothing and then quickly return to her play.

Insecure-Avoidant

Jared, 50 months old, abruptly leaves the art area after jabbing playdough with a plastic carving tool until it is torn apart. He enters the water table area and pushes between two children to get to the water. Both of the children he pushes tell him to stop, but he persists. Jared takes a toy boat and drops it from as high as he can reach. The boat's splash gets the other children wet. The children, angry at Jared, again tell him to stop; one child cries. Jared replies, "It's just water, crybaby!"

Before the teacher can reach him, he runs to the block area where Marissa and Alex are playing. The teacher calls Jared's name, but he ignores her. As soon as Jared reaches the blocks, he grabs the toy airplane that Alex just put on his newly constructed airport runway and states, "I need this."

Jared demonstrates how a child with an insecure-avoidant attachment pattern might engage in free play in an early childhood setting. Jared's play explorations are superficial and focused more on objects than on people. Socially, children like Jared may appear to teachers and peers as extremely independent. They tend to play alone, engaging in parallel play even through the preschool years. When they do interact with peers, children with insecure-avoidant attachment tend to show more hostile and rejecting behavior than do other children. In fact, children with insecure-avoidant attachment may intentionally taunt or bully others for no apparent reason.

Though they may appear to be indifferent, many children who have an insecure-avoidant attachment pattern are suppressing feelings of fear and anxiety. Some may have challenges with their attachment figures (i.e., primary caregivers), such as parents working long hours, suffering from an illness, or providing insufficient attention that might result in the child often feeling alone during times of distress. When interacting with others, these children may use avoidance as a defense strategy. They may have difficulty playing cooperatively, making friends, and sustaining friendships over time (Dunn 2004). Not surprisingly, they tend to experience high rates of peer rejection (Dunn 2004). Social, emotional, and academic learning may be hindered for children with insecure-avoidant attachment because they generally do not have the emotional reserves to engage in socially complex play. Their overall demeanor says, "I'm alone in this world. Things are safer than people."

Insecure-Ambivalent

Tessa, 48 months old, arrives at her classroom with her mother. Tessa clings to her mother's arm as her mother puts Tessa's blankie in her cubby. Tessa's teacher, Ms. Jamil, invites her to join an art activity, but Tessa hides behind her mother.

When her mother leaves, Tessa retreats to a beanbag chair in the book area. Lying on the beanbag, she holds her blankie in one hand and a baby doll that she retrieved from the dramatic play area in the other. When other children come into the book area, she watches them but does not interact.

Later, Tessa ventures into the rest of the room but doesn't move freely. She prefers to stay close to Ms. Jamil, quietly following the teacher around while clutching her doll. Tessa seems especially vigilant about the front door and startles when the door opens or closes.

Tessa demonstrates how a child with an insecure-ambivalent attachment pattern might behave during free play. Tessa's fear makes it difficult for her to explore. Children with insecure-ambivalent attachment typically either stay in one location, playing with toys immediately within that location, or follow the caregiver. Because these children do not engage in play that their peers find interesting, their peers tend to avoid them or even tease them (McElwain & Volling 2004). When facilitating interaction,

teachers should be intentional and attentive, as some research has found that children with insecure-ambivalent attachment were sometimes mistreated during peer play when paired with peers with insecure-avoidant attachment (Sroufe 1989).

Unlike insecure-avoidant children, insecure-ambivalent children usually do not fear rejection, yet they tend not to expect their caregivers to be capable of soothing them. They often have extreme difficulty separating from primary caregivers and recovering from being upset. Teachers' attempts to comfort them are often met with bids for attention, like sulking, pouting, or other displays of helplessness. They may be irritable for no apparent reason and hard to console. Children with insecure-ambivalent attachment might be unable to work through difficult tasks. They can be demanding, easily frustrated, and impatient with others' offers to assist. Their overall demeanor says, "The world is an uncertain place. I need to keep watch."

Meeting the Needs of Insecure Children: Recommendations for Early Childhood Educators

The relationships teachers have with the children in their care are crucial to the children's development (Gerber, Whitebook, & Weinstein 2007). In fact, the quality of teacher-child relationships is a strong predictor of children's future academic, social, and emotional functioning (Sabol & Pianta 2012). Research has shown that it is possible for young children to form secure attachments with educators and for high-quality teachers to buffer environmental risks experienced by young children (Dinehart et al. 2012). Through responsive caregiving, adults can alter their own behavior to meet children's emotional needs, thereby enhancing the attachment relationship (Hong & Park 2012). Teachers' understanding of play behaviors can increase their intentionality and responsiveness.

It is important to remember that children's behaviors communicate their needs. Children with challenging behavior are calling for adults' attention, care, and support. The following suggestions can help teachers provide an environment that supports children's individual needs.

1. **Increase time engaged in one-on-one warm, positive interactions,** especially with children whose behaviors are either withdrawn or aggressive (Pianta 1999). For 5 to 15 minutes each day, give the child your undivided attention, allowing the child to guide play. Narrate what you see the child doing, conveying acceptance and interest while being sensitive and patient.

2. **Provide time and support for children's imaginative and creative play.** Children with challenging play behaviors, in particular, need ample opportunity to practice play skills. Teachers can support those children in engaging in dramatic play and in expanding their play to involve other children. The children may need suggestions for how objects can be used in dramatic play (such as using a circular tube as a steering wheel). They may need encouragement to take risks in novel situations. Take time to observe the children and ask them about what they are doing while acknowledging and encouraging instances of imaginative play.

3. **Scaffold children's play interactions.**
Focus on scaffolding experiences of mutual engagement and enjoyment. Remember, a child who has difficulty playing with others, like Jared, may have learned that it is best to avoid interactions; the key is to express interest in that child's play. For example, if the child is throwing blocks into a bucket, you can start to build a small tower nearby and narrate what you are doing. Initially, your goal may simply be for the child to imitate you. Later on, try to transition to playing together when the child seems more comfortable.

Over time, increase expressions of affection, both verbally ("I am really enjoying my time with you") and nonverbally (smiling). If the child does not respond to these overtures, continue to engage, extending the length of turn taking each time. Once the child becomes more able to engage, introduce a peer into the interaction. After the child has been successful in several peer interactions, slowly remove yourself and continue to observe. (See "Helping Tessa Enjoy Playing with Other Children.")

4. **Strive for connection, not correction.**
Connection occurs when we let go of the need to control a child's behavior and instead focus on the reason behind the behavior. Unfortunately, teachers often resort to using punitive strategies with children who exhibit challenging behavior (Sabol & Pianta 2012). While immediate teacher intervention is often necessary for physical and emotional safety, immediate punishment may not be the best strategy.

Punitive strategies may address the immediate behavior (e.g., the child might stop throwing sand at other children), but they do not address the child's unmet need that is driving the behavior (e.g., wanting to enter play but not knowing how). Challenging behavior (such as Jared's in the second vignette) is often "less an act of defiance and more an indication of his inner chaos" (Tsabary 2013, 98). When we see a child's behavior as communication of needs, we can begin to explore ways to relate to the child, to truly be with the child, and to support the process of the child connecting to another person.

5. **Be a reflective teacher.** Personal reflection, especially when a child's behavior causes you stress, is critical to responding in supportive ways. Reflective teaching means that teachers are willing to look at what they do in the classroom, think about why they do it, and think about what the children are learning (Eggbeer, Shahmoon-Shanok, & Clark 2010).

Helping Tessa Enjoy Playing with Other Children

Children like Tessa, who often depend on the teacher to be next to them when they are playing, may show signs of jealousy when the teacher gives attention to other children. Teachers can help these children develop a sense of autonomy in their play by breaking down play into small steps. For example, Tessa's teacher could narrate what she sees Tessa doing: "You are holding the doll tightly with your hands." The teacher could then ask permission to join in the play alongside the child. The teacher may also introduce new props—such as a cup, plate, and spoon—and invite Tessa to feed the doll with her.

As the play becomes more elaborate, other children may want to join. At first, limit it to one other child so that the child with insecure behaviors can ease into social interactions. After two or three play sessions in which you sit with the child, say to the child that you need to help someone else, and that you will be right back. Follow through, checking back after a few minutes. Gradually increase the amount of time that you leave the child until they show more confidence playing with others on their own. The more encouragement you offer the child about their growing independence (e.g., "I noticed how you and Katie were playing house together!"), the more comfortable and desirable such actions will be to the child.

At the core of reflective practice is teachers' willingness to know themselves. With regard to attachment, this means knowing how your background and values might influence how you respond to children. What are your own attachment histories? Do certain attachment behaviors draw you toward or away from children?

Reflective practice is also empathetic. When we are reflective, we look at situations from the child's perspective (Carter et al. 2010). We ask questions like, "Why might the child be having such a difficult time separating from their parent?" and "What social and emotional themes is the child exploring in their dramatic play?" Finding answers may require getting more information from the child's family. Although we may not be able to explicitly ask about attachment histories, we can ask about any behavioral concerns that the family may have. To close one reflective cycle and begin another, teachers should "make effective, meaningful decisions about how to respond to and plan for children" (Carter et al. 2010, 18).

6. **Give the child's inner experiences a voice during play by using language that describes emotions.** Whether anxious like Tessa or avoidant like Jared, children who feel insecure often harbor a sense of rejection. As the child plays, teachers can use emotional vocabulary to help the child put words to their experiences, both positive and negative.

While all children need support in learning words to describe the full spectrum of emotions, some children may benefit from added support in using words for negative emotions—such as *frustration, disappointment,* and *anger*—to learn to describe their feelings. During dramatic play, for example, one child might have their doll grab a toy from another child's doll; the teacher might say, "I can see that this doll is feeling really angry that the other doll grabbed the toy."

When teachers provide children with emotional labels, they are coregulating the children's intense emotions. With consistent support, children gradually learn to regulate their emotions on their own (Siegel & Bryson 2012).

Reflection Questions

1. Are strong relationships necessary for successful play interactions? How would such relationships serve as a protective factor for young children?

2. Supporting children's friendship skills often requires understanding underlying factors that may impact peer relationships. As a teacher, how do you identify and respond to these factors?

3. With your teaching team, identify one of the seven recommendations included in this article that you could embed throughout the day. What are three ways you can put this recommendation into practice with children in your classroom?

4. Reflect on what you have learned from reading this article. How does it change your perceptions of young children's challenging behavior? How will you respond differently to challenging behavior in the future?

7. **Help children develop empathy during play.** Children may need help recognizing how their behaviors impact others. To help children develop empathy, teachers can first model these skills during free play and storybook reading. Teachers can use phrases like, "I think she feels . . ." or "His expression tells me he is feeling . . . ." Connecting "When . . . , then . . ." is also useful in teaching perspective. Recall Jared grabbing Alex's toy airplane. Before jumping into problem-solving mode, the teacher could say to Jared, "When you grab a toy from a friend, then they feel really sad."

Conclusion

All children come to early childhood settings wanting to connect with others and to learn, but many children have not yet developed the emotional security necessary for being receptive to new learning experiences. Teachers have an important role in helping all children feel safe. Children who have insecure attachment histories are at particular risk for a host of poor outcomes, including not performing well in school and social and emotional maladjustment (Hamre & Pianta 2001). By observing children's play, teachers can begin to understand children's behavior and identify possible avenues for intervention. Through play, teachers can create new, more positive relational experiences for young children that can benefit all aspects of their well-being.

REFERENCES

Ainsworth, M.D.S., M.C. Blehar, E. Waters, & S.N. Wall. 1978. *Patterns of Attachment: A Psychological Study of the Strange Situation.* Hillsdale, NJ: Erlbaum.

Behrens, K.Y., E. Hesse, & M. Main. 2007. "Mothers' Attachment Status as Determined by the Adult Attachment Interview Predicts Their 6-Year-Olds' Reunion Responses: A Study Conducted in Japan." *Developmental Psychology* 43 (6): 1553–67.

Bowlby, J. (1969) 1983. *Attachment.* Vol. 1 of *Attachment and Loss.* New York: Basic Books.

Carter, M., W. Cividanes, D. Curtis, & D. Lebo. 2010. "Becoming a Reflective Teacher." *Teaching Young Children* 3 (4): 18–20.

Dinehart, L.H., L.F. Katz, L. Manfra, & M.A. Ullery. 2012. "Providing Quality Early Care and Education to Young Children Who Experience Maltreatment: A Review of the Literature." *Early Childhood Education Journal* 41 (4): 283–90.

Dunn, J. 2004. *Children's Friendships: The Beginnings of Intimacy.* Understanding Children's Worlds series. Malden, MA: Blackwell.

Eggbeer, L., R. Shahmoon-Shanok, & R. Clark. 2010. "Reaching Toward an Evidence Base for Reflective Supervision." *ZERO TO THREE* 31 (2): 39–45.

Gerber, E.B., M. Whitebook, & R.S. Weinstein. 2007. "At the Heart of Child Care: Predictors of Teacher Sensitivity in Center-Based Child Care." *Early Childhood Research Quarterly* 22 (3): 327–46.

Hamre, B.K., & R.C. Pianta. 2001. "Early Teacher-Child Relationships and the Trajectory of Children's School Outcomes Through Eighth Grade." *Child Development* 72 (2): 625–38.

Hong, Y.R., & J.S. Park. 2012. "Impact of Attachment, Temperament, and Parenting on Human Development." *Korean Journal of Pediatrics* 55 (12): 449–54.

McElwain, N.L., & B.L. Volling. 2004. "Attachment Security and Parental Sensitivity During Infancy: Associations with Friendship Quality and False-Belief Understanding at Age 4." *Journal of Social and Personal Relationships* 21 (5): 639–67.

Piaget, J., & B. Inhelder. 1962. *The Psychology of the Child.* New York: Basic.

Pianta, R.C. 1999. *Enhancing Relationships Between Children and Teachers.* Washington, DC: American Psychological Association.

Raby, K.L., G.I. Roisman, R.C. Fraley, & J.A. Simpson. 2015. "The Enduring Predictive Significance of Early Maternal Sensitivity: Social and Academic Competence Through Age 32 Years." *Child Development* 86 (3): 695–708.

Sabol, T.J., & R.C. Pianta. 2012. "Recent Trends in Research on Teacher–Child Relationships." *Attachment & Human Development* 14 (3): 213–31.

Schore, A.N. 2001. "Effects of a Secure Attachment Relationship on Right Brain Development, Affect Regulation, and Infant Mental Health." *Infant Mental Health Journal* 22 (1–2): 7–66.

Siegel, D.J., & T.P Bryson. 2012. *The Whole-Brain Child: 12 Revolutionary Strategies to Nurture Your Child's Developing Mind.* New York: Bantam.

Silver, R.B., J.R. Measelle, J.M. Armstrong, & M.J. Essex. 2005. "Trajectories of Classroom Externalizing Behavior: Contributions of Child Characteristics, Family Characteristics, and the Teacher–Child Relationship During the School Transition." *Journal of School Psychology* 43 (1): 39–60.

Spilt, J.L., & H.M.Y. Koomen. 2009. "Widening the View on Teacher–Child Relationships: Teachers' Narratives Concerning Disruptive Versus Nondisruptive Children." *School Psychology Review* 38 (1): 86–101.

Sroufe, L.A. 1989. "Pathways to Adaptation and Maladaptation: Psychopathology as Developmental Deviation." Chap. 2 in *The Emergence of a Discipline: Rochester Symposium on Developmental Psychopathology,* ed. D. Cicchetti, vol. 1, 13–40. Hillsdale, NJ: Erlbaum.

Sroufe, L.A. 2005. "Attachment and Development: A Prospective, Longitudinal Study from Birth to Adulthood." *Attachment and Human Development* 7 (4): 349–67.

Thompson, R.A. 2008. "Early Attachment and Later Development: Familiar Questions, New Answers." In *Handbook of Attachment: Theory, Research, and Clinical Applications,* 2nd ed., eds. J. Cassidy & P.R. Shaver, 348–65. New York: Guilford.

Tsabary, S. 2013. *Out of Control: Why Disciplining Your Child Doesn't Work and What Will.* Vancouver, BC: Namaste.

Wismer Fries, A.B., T.E. Ziegler, J.R. Kurian, S. Jacoris, & S.D. Pollak. 2005. "Early Experience in Humans Is Associated with Changes in Neuropeptides Critical for Regulating Social Behavior." *Proceedings of the National Academy of Sciences* 102 (47): 17237–40.

About the Authors

Shulamit N. Ritblatt, PhD, is professor emerita in the department of Child and Family Development at San Diego State University. Dr. Ritblatt is an expert in early childhood social and emotional development with a focus on early childhood mental health and learning readiness. Her work focuses on prevention and early intervention, utilizing relational, reflective, and trauma-informed practices to support healthy development of children and their families and to enhance family engagement in education.

Sascha Longstreth, PhD, is interim department chair and associate professor of Child and Family Development at San Diego State University. She began her career as a preschool teacher and has extensive experience in a variety of educational settings. She serves as codirector of the Center for Excellence in Early Development, a transdisciplinary, research-based training facility with a holistic approach to supporting early childhood development, mental health, and early childhood education in San Diego County and beyond.

Outdoor Recess Matters!

Preventing and Reducing Children's Challenging Behavior on the Playground

Hsiu-Wen Yang, Michaelene M. Ostrosky, Paddy Cronin Favazza, Yusuf Akemoğlu, W. Catherine Cheung, and Katherine Aronson-Ensign

Ocean School is an inclusive, full-day preschool in a college town. The school houses approximately 150 students, ages 3 to 5. Each of the 10 multiage classes has 15 children, two to five of whom have identified disabilities. Children at Ocean School have a typical preschool schedule that includes 60 minutes of unstructured recess each day. If the weather is good, teachers take their classes to the playground. In the extreme cold or rain, children have recess in a gym that is equipped with balls, scooters, Hula Hoops, and other indoor gross motor materials.

Elanor has taught at Ocean School for almost two years. She knows her children enjoy outdoor recess time. The playground is an ideal setting for them to socialize and to develop friendship skills. Yet Elanor has encountered many behavioral issues on the playground. For example, last week she observed two children fighting over a bike; she saw one child push another aside to be first in line for the slide; and she noticed multiple children engaging in unsafe use of the playground equipment. Elanor warned the children that if they did not play appropriately, their recess time would be shortened or canceled altogether. However, these behaviors continue to occur, and she is losing patience as she finds herself constantly reprimanding children. Elanor is at a loss for what to do to reduce these behavior issues and has started to question her skills as a teacher.

Early childhood programs should provide children with daily recess for active play (NAECS-SDE 2001). The US Department of Health and Human Services recommends that preschoolers engage in at least 60 minutes of structured and 60 minutes of unstructured physical activity each day (Piercy & Troiano 2018). Typically, recess occurs outside on the school playground. During this time, children take a short break from more structured instruction to play and explore independently, socialize with peers, and enjoy physical activities. Professional guidelines stress that recess should not be withheld as a punishment; likewise, educators should not reduce or eliminate it for children who need extra support to meet behavioral expectations (NAEYC 2020).

Spending time on the playground is a great opportunity for children to be physically active and engage in various forms of play. Moreover, the unstructured, self-directed nature of playground environments can help children develop a variety of foundational social and emotional skills. These skills include self-regulation, showing empathy, talking about emotions, engaging in positive peer and adult interactions, and cooperating with others.

Yet while offering time and space for active, engaged play, the playground also is a setting that is ripe for challenging behavior like hitting, pushing, arguing, and playing in an unsafe way (Brez & Sheets 2017; Mulryan-Kyne 2014). These behaviors can occur due to unclear expectations, varied skill levels, and a lack of structured routines. Emerging social and emotional skills also can contribute to problematic behaviors. In particular, some children with disabilities or children with delays in the social domain may require more support to follow rules, be included in activities, solve problems, initiate peer interaction, or engage in motor play (Anderson et al. 2004; McNamara et al. 2018).

Responding to challenging behavior can be difficult for many teachers (Westling 2010), especially in unstructured settings. As professionals with extensive experience teaching young children with and without disabilities and preparing future early childhood and early childhood special education teachers, we have noticed a high frequency of behaviors similar to what Elanor observed during recess. We have seen the frustrations these behaviors elicit, including teachers questioning their competence and abilities. In this article, we share strategies that can be easily implemented before, during, and after recess to promote social and emotional competence and to prevent challenging behavior among preschool children. Our recommendations are based on the pyramid model, a framework for supporting social and emotional competence for young children (Hemmeter, Ostrosky, & Fox 2021). Teachers can use the recommendations shared in this article to enhance recess experiences for all children.

Strategies for Preventing and Addressing Challenging Behavior on the Playground

Elanor decides to discuss her frustrations with Lily, who has taught at Ocean School for over 10 years. Lily shares some ideas and strategies that she has learned from attending several training workshops on the pyramid model. She also recommends online resources from recognized sources (see page 53) that she believes might help prevent some behavioral problems on the playground.

When managing challenging behavior, teachers are encouraged to promote children's positive behaviors rather than use exclusionary tactics like timeouts. The pyramid model (which can be viewed at www.challengingbehavior.org/pyramid-model/overview/tiers) includes evidence-based strategies and a three-tiered system of supports to promote children's social and emotional development and to prevent and address challenging behavior (Hemmeter, Ostrosky, & Fox 2021). These tiers are

> Universal practices, which include building positive relationships and creating supportive environments

> Targeted social and emotional supports

> Intensive individualized interventions

An underlying premise of the model is that addressing the first two tiers of practice can meet the majority of children's needs, leaving only a few students needing intensive individualized support. Here, we outline the first two tiers, defining each and sharing specific ways that educators can connect to them. The final tier requires more individualization and is beyond the scope of this article. (Refer to Artman-Meeker et al. 2021 and Fox, Dunlap, & Ferro 2021 for more information on the top tier.)

Universal Practices: Building Positive Relationships

The foundation of the pyramid model is building positive and supportive relationships—not only with children, but also with families. Children who enjoy supportive relationships with adults are more responsive to them and more likely to cooperate, follow directions, and develop self-confidence (Fox et al. 2003).

To help build these relationships, we encourage teachers to regularly move around the playground and to actively engage with children while supervising their safety. This is in contrast to the frequently observed practice of teachers standing to the side and predominantly observing children at play. To increase their engagement, teachers can

> Get down on children's level and make eye contact with them

> Engage in conversations around children's topics of interest by asking open-ended questions ("What ball games do you know?"; "Who is your favorite baseball player?")

> Provide descriptive praise and encouragement by acknowledging children's efforts ("Jerry, you made it halfway across the monkey bars! That's awesome!")

In addition, building meaningful and caring relationships with families may help educators understand, plan for, and reduce children's challenging behavior. We encourage teachers to invest time in communicating and connecting with families. One way to do this is to ask families to complete an interest survey about their children's favorite outdoor activities (see "Sample Interest Survey" on page 47). This survey is designed to garner children's input; teachers can use it to learn about children's interests and to plan highly engaging recess activities. They also can use it to ask families about behaviors they see at home and strategies that teachers might employ to address challenging behavior at school.

Universal Practices: Creating Supportive Environments

Children are more likely to exhibit challenging behavior in unstructured settings (like a playground) because the environment is unpredictable, and children may not know what is expected of them (Akers et al. 2016). The pyramid model focuses on creating predictable and supportive learning environments to decrease the likelihood of challenging behavior and to promote positive child outcomes. These outcomes include successful peer interaction, engagement, and social and emotional development. Because the environment plays such a critical role in children's behavior, teachers can implement the following strategies to ensure that the playground is a supportive one. Additionally, teachers can scaffold a child's learning and development through strategies such as prompting, modeling, or adapting materials or activities. This support and scaffolding can be provided during planned as well as naturally occurring activities (NAEYC 2020).

Teach Expectations and Ground Rules

On the playground, teachers expect children to follow directions, take turns, and play safely. However, for many children, these expectations must be taught explicitly, intentionally, and systematically. Teachers can start this process by creating playground-related lesson plans with the following components:

> Define the rules and discuss appropriate and inappropriate playground behaviors to help children know what is expected of them (Franzen & Kamps 2008). For instance, in the opening vignette, Elanor could prepare children to take turns on the limited number of bikes by bringing a timer outside and encouraging children to set it each time they take a turn. This way, multiple children will be able to ride the bikes during recess.

> Help children understand why the rules are important and need to be followed (Binder, Lentini, & Steed 2021). During morning meeting, Elanor might engage children in a discussion about what could happen if they run up the slide or stand on it, emphasizing how unsafe these behaviors are.

> Demonstrate examples of both appropriate and inappropriate behaviors within learning experiences to increase children's participation and engagement (Ennis, Schwab, & Jolivette 2012). During small group time, Elanor might share stories of appropriate versus inappropriate behaviors (e.g., children pushing other children while waiting in line to go down the slide versus standing an arm's length behind the person in front of them). She can then have children vote on which example is safe.

> During planned experiences, provide opportunities for children to practice adhering and not adhering to expectations through role-play (Ennis, Schwab, & Jolivette 2012). As children do this, teachers can encourage them to identify and give feedback about examples of appropriate and inappropriate

Sample Interest Survey

My child's name is _____

Instruction
Please work with your child to identify their favorite outdoor activities.
Circle the smiling face if your child likes the activity; circle the frowning face
if they do not.

I like to play:

😊 ☹️   😊 ☹️   😊 ☹️

😊 ☹️   😊 ☹️   😊 ☹️

Please share the following information with your child's teacher:

Tell me what might frustrate your child when playing on the playground.

_____

_____

What strategies or materials might help your child calm down if they
become upset on the playground?

_____

_____

actions, words, or choices. For example, as two children demonstrate playing with a ball and refusing to let a third child join their game, peers can identify why this is not appropriate and how they should invite the child to join them instead.

> Ask open-ended questions to check children's understanding of playground expectations (Test, Cunningham, & Lee 2010). Elanor can do this after talking about playground equipment safety by asking questions such as "If you stand on the swing, what might happen?"

To increase their impact, playground expectations and rules should initially be taught at the beginning of the school year (Leedy, Bates, & Safran 2004). Teachers can provide opportunities for children to review and try them out (with support and feedback as needed) throughout the year (Todd et al. 2002). For an example of a playground-related learning experience, see "Lesson Plan: Using Playground Equipment Safely."

Lesson Plan: Using Playground Equipment Safely

Objective	Children will learn how to use the playground equipment correctly and play safely.
Context	Classroom and playground
Time	Classroom, 20 minutes; playground, 20 minutes
Materials	> Pictures of all the playground equipment. > Playground safety worksheet (including visuals with different playground actions, such as a child sitting or standing on the swing). Educators can search for pictures online. > Whiteboard, poster board, or chart paper divided into two sides, one labeled "safe" and one labeled "not safe."
Introduction	"Today we are going to talk about why it is important to keep everyone safe on the playground." > Discuss why we must keep everyone safe while playing on the playground (i.e., to prevent playground injuries; so everyone can have fun).

Activities	1. Discuss the rules for using the playground equipment. (Location: classroom)
	
	    > Show pictures of the playground equipment and introduce each item (swings, slides, seesaw, sandbox).
	    > Ask children to describe the correct ways to use each piece of equipment.
	    > With children's input, place a variety of pictures cut from the safety worksheet in the *safe* or *not safe* column on a whiteboard, poster board, or chart paper. As the pictures are sorted, discuss why these are safe versus unsafe ways to use the equipment.
	
	2. Practice safe ways to use the playground equipment. (Location: playground)
	
	    > Visit each piece of equipment and model correct ways to use it (e.g., "I am going to show you the safe ways to play on the swing. I want you to watch me carefully.")
	    > Model some incorrect ways to use the equipment and make it clear what behaviors children should engage in that are safe (e.g., "We don't stand on the swing; we remain seated because we could fall and hurt ourselves.")
	    > Give children about 10 minutes to play and practice safe playground behaviors.
	    > Observe children's behaviors. Provide behavior-specific feedback if needed.
	    > Ask questions and make sure that children understand the expectations for playground safety (e.g., "How should you play on the swing?")

Sorting Playground Behavior

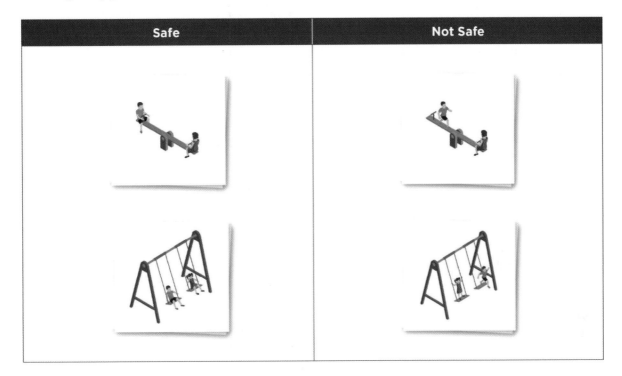

Safe	Not Safe

Provide Prompts and Cues

After introducing and practicing rules, we encourage teachers to review them with children before entering the playground. To meet the needs of all children, teachers can remind them of rules in multiple ways. For instance, as Elanor approaches the Ocean School playground, she might say, "Remember, you need to stay seated on the swings"—an auditory reminder. She might hang poster or chart paper in her room or on the door leading to the playground with pictures that depict safe and unsafe behaviors—a visual reminder (Evanovich & Kern 2018). (See "Sorting Playground Behavior" for an example of this.) For children who need additional scaffolding, Elanor can create portable visual supports, such as laminated photos on a keyring that match the materials on the playground.

Employ Teacher-Guided Play

Some children may benefit from participating in teacher-guided play activities during outdoor recess. This is especially helpful when children are learning new play behaviors. Using the principles of universal design for learning (UDL), educators can work to proactively provide multiple means of engagement, action, and expression on the playground (Horn et al. 2016; NAEYC 2020) by

> Introducing games over the course of several days

> Using visual supports to reinforce the rules of play

> Providing positive, descriptive feedback ("You patiently waited in line, then sat when you went down the slide! Well done!")

> Encouraging respectful peer engagement ("I like the way you asked for a turn with the bean bags" or "That is great that you helped your friend get the bowling ball.")

One resource to support teachers is *CHAMPPS: CHildren in Action Motor Program for PreschoolerS*, a grant-funded motor play program developed by the authors (Favazza et al. 2023). It contains many UDL-infused strategies for gross motor play that are ideal for inclusive preschool settings.

Targeted Social and Emotional Supports

Individualization is a key component of both the pyramid model and developmentally appropriate practice. Teachers must constantly look for ways to be responsive to and "accommodate the range of children's individual differences in development, language, skills and abilities, prior experiences, needs, and interests" (NAEYC 2020, 21).

While the majority of children's needs can be met by building relationships and creating quality environments, some children may need more explicit instruction and support to successfully navigate time on the playground. These can include teaching them how to express and regulate their emotions, how to play cooperatively, how to develop friendship skills, and how to solve problems (Fox et al. 2010). Following are specific strategies to support such skill development during recess.

Pair Playground Friends

Children with social delays are less likely to initiate social interaction and often end up being excluded by their peers (Anderson et al. 2004). Likewise, some children without disabilities or delays are shy, withdrawn, or still developing critical social skills. Assigning peer partners (e.g., for a bowling game or to play hockey outdoors) who rotate on a regular basis can help children acquire friendship skills and provide them with multiple opportunities for social interaction (Meyer, Milan, & Ostrosky 2021). To prepare peer partners, teachers can create lists of children with strong social skills, then pair them—using matching stickers or necklaces—with children who would benefit from more support. (See Meyer, Milan, & Ostrosky 2021 for additional strategies that teachers can use to teach friendship skills.)

Include Gross Motor Books in the Classroom

Teachers can read interactive motor books that emphasize cooperative play instead of competition. This will help reinforce skill development on the playground and social and emotional learning while also supporting language and literacy (Favazza et al. 2023). These books can be used to teach children how to move in new ways, play appropriately with peers, and maintain a safe environment.

For example, in the book *Jump!* by Steve Lavis, children can practice jumping like a tiger, swinging like a monkey, slithering like a snake, flying like a toucan, and stomping like an elephant. Likewise, in *Dance with Me*, by Charles R. Smith Jr., illustrated by Noah Z. Jones, children are prompted to dance, twist, wiggle, bounce, shake, and twirl. They can do these moves independently or with partners to encourage peer interaction.

Include Social and Emotional Learning Games

Many young children are learning to identify feelings, cope with their feelings, and play cooperatively. To maximize the social and emotional benefits that can occur while playing on the playground, teachers can create and implement learning games to facilitate cooperation and peer socialization. "Social and Emotional Learning Activities and Strategies" provides examples of how teachers can do this.

Social and Emotional Learning Activities and Strategies

Strategy	Activities	
	Throw and catch the ball (pair, small group)	**Bottle bowling (pair, small group)**
Recognize and describe emotions	Ask children, "How do you feel when you catch the ball?"	Ask children, "How do you feel when you knock all the pins down?" Ask children, "How do you feel when you miss the pins?"
Solve and/or prevent problems	Establish rules (e.g., don't overthrow balls on purpose) and demonstrate correct and incorrect ways to throw the ball.	Establish rules by saying, "Let's roll the ball safely!" and "Stay in your personal space!" Demonstrate correct and incorrect ways to roll the ball and knock over the pins.
Take turns and wait for a turn	Remind children to watch and wait to retrieve the ball.	Remind children to watch and wait to retrieve the ball.
Help and support peers	Ask children, "Who can help pass out the balls?"	Ask children to retrieve the ball for their partner.
Play cooperatively	Encourage children to throw and catch the ball with their partner.	Ask children to help their partner set up the pins.
Share materials	Encourage children to ask a classmate to exchange balls.	Pair children to share the bowling station.
Socialize with peers	Encourage children to call their partner's name while passing the ball. For example, "Nora, here comes the ball!"	Ask children to cheer on their partner as they bowl.

Adapted, by permission, from P.C. Favazza & M.M. Ostrosky, with M. Stalega, H.-W. Yang, K. Aronson-Ensign, M. Block, W.C. Cheung, & Y. Akemoğlu, *CHAMPPS: CHildren in Action Motor Program for PreschoolerS* (Baltimore: Brookes, 2023).

After-Recess Strategies

We have suggested several strategies that teachers can use to promote social and emotional skills and to prevent challenging behavior before and during outdoor recess. Next, we share a few strategies that teachers can use to support and expand what children are learning into class routines after recess time.

Reinforce Children's Positive Choices

While children line up and get ready to transition back to their classrooms, teachers can reinforce their positive behaviors and choices by giving a high-five, thumbs up, elbow bump, or other form of physical reinforcement. They also can provide positive, descriptive feedback. For instance, Elanor might give Shana an elbow bump and comment, "Shana, I like the way you asked Ying for the beach ball. Ying really likes to play with you." (For more information about using positive, descriptive feedback, see Conroy & Sutherland 2021).

Use Book Nooks to Expand on Social and Emotional Skills

To expand on what children are learning about playground expectations, teachers can select and read books that focus on social and emotional development (such as *I Can Share!* by Karen Katz). Then, they can create discussion questions and activities to expand on what children are learning on the playground. For instance, Elanor could ask questions like "How did you share the bikes with your friends?" while reading the story. She could also prepare props that represent playground equipment and toys and have children demonstrate how to share them. (For Book Nook ideas, see www.challengingbehavior.org/collection/book-nook.)

Highlight Friendship Behaviors in the Classroom

To encourage children's friendship skills within the classroom, teachers can take digital pictures to capture friendship behaviors on the playground (e.g., children pushing each other on the swings, children taking turns with bikes). These pictures can be used to support and advance children's mastery of friendship skills by displaying them on a bulletin board, the classroom wall, or in a classroom book. For example, when adding a photo to her classroom "Friendship Book," Elanor might ask Travis, "Tell me about this photo of you pushing Roy on the swings." Elanor could then write Travis's words underneath the photo in the book.

Conclusion

After talking with Lily and exploring pyramid model resources, Elanor cannot wait to try some new strategies during outdoor recess. First, she sends an interest survey to families, tailoring it to include all of the equipment and activities available on Ocean School's playground. Then she creates a playground lesson plan that includes talking with children about the safe behaviors they need to exhibit on the playground, such as taking turns.

Once on the playground, Elanor walks around it, regularly getting down on the children's level to talk about what they are doing and frequently asking what playground activities they like. She reinforces their interactions with comments such as, "It looks like you are having fun with your friends!" When she notices a few children lining up for their turn on the slide, she acknowledges their appropriate behaviors by saying, "I like the way you are waiting with your friends for a turn!" When Elanor sees two children arguing and pushing each other for a turn on the tire swing, she steps forward and reminds them that they need to take turns.

After a few weeks, Elanor notices that most of the children in her class are engaging in appropriate playground behaviors and following the rules. However, she also observes some children who need additional support. She initiates peer pairings and plans some activities to support each child's social and emotional development.

After implementing these strategies for two months, Elanor notices a significant decrease in challenging behavior and an increase in social and emotional skills. Moreover, she is more confident every time she takes her class to the playground.

Pyramid Model Resources

More information about the pyramid model can be found at

> National Center for Pyramid Model Innovations, **www.challengingbehavior.org**

> *Unpacking the Pyramid Model: A Practical Guide for Preschool Teachers* (2021), edited by Mary Louise Hemmeter, Michaelene M. Ostrosky, and Lise Fox

Resources on social and emotional development can be found at the Early Childhood Learning & Knowledge Center, US Department of Health and Human Services Administration for Children and Families, **https://eclkc.ohs.acf.hhs.gov/browse/keyword/social-emotional-development**.

Reflection Questions

1. What do you have in place to maintain a balance between structured and unstructured outdoor activities and to proactively prevent challenging behavior?

2. Reflect on some of the challenges in your particular program and what considerations are necessary. What is one strategy from this article you could implement to prevent challenging behavior in your outdoor space?

3. How might children help to develop the rules for outdoor recess?

4. How might you use information from an interest survey to plan engaging activities and promote communication and self-regulation?

5. What might be key opportunities to target social and emotional development during outdoor recess?

Recess is an important component of early childhood education, yet still emerging social and emotional skills can negatively affect children's engagement and behavior. After reading this article, early childhood educators can reflect on their own practices by

> Writing down three to five strategies that they already use to support children's playground behavior. Then reflect: What behaviors do they notice on the playground? Are their supports working? What should they consider changing?

> Writing down strategies that they would like to try. What are the next steps? What do they need in order to implement these strategies?

> Monitoring children's playground behavior. As educators notice changes, they should consider ways to celebrate successes and positive behavioral outcomes.

REFERENCES

Akers, J.S., T.S. Higbee, J.S. Pollard, A.J. Pellegrino, & K.R. Gerencser. 2016. "An Evaluation of Photographic Activity Schedules to Increase Independent Playground Skills in Young Children with Autism." *Journal of Applied Behavior Analysis* 49 (4): 954–59.

Artman-Meeker, K., E.E. Barton, P.S. Strain, & M.L. Hemmeter. 2021. "Understanding, Preventing, and Responding to Challenging Behavior." In *Unpacking the Pyramid Model: A Practical Guide for Preschool Teachers*, eds. M.L. Hemmeter, M.M. Ostrosky, & L. Fox, 141–50. Baltimore: Brookes.

Anderson, A., D.W. Moore, R. Godfrey, & C.M. Fletcher-Flinn. 2004. "Social Skills Assessment of Children with Autism in Free-Play Situations." *Autism* 8 (4): 369–85.

Binder, D.P., R. Lentini, & E.A. Steed. 2021. "Teaching Expectations and Rules." In *Unpacking the Pyramid Model: A Practical Guide for Preschool Teachers*, eds. M.L. Hemmeter, M.M. Ostrosky, & L. Fox, 71–80. Baltimore: Brookes.

Brez, C., & V. Sheets. 2017. "Classroom Benefits of Recess." *Learning Environments Research* 20 (3): 433–45.

Conroy, M.A., & K.S. Sutherland. 2021. "Using Positive Descriptive Feedback to Improve Children's Behavior." In *Unpacking the Pyramid Model: A Practical Guide for Preschool Teachers*, eds. M.L. Hemmeter, M.M. Ostrosky, & L. Fox, 101–08. Baltimore: Brookes.

Ennis, R.P., J.R. Schwab, & K. Jolivette. 2012. "Using Precorrection as a Secondary-Tier Intervention for Reducing Problem Behaviors in Instructional and Noninstructional Settings." *Beyond Behavior* 22 (1): 40–47.

Evanovich, L.L., & L. Kern. 2018. "Precorrection: Preventing Predictable Problem Behaviors in School Settings." *Beyond Behavior* 27 (2): 90–98.

Favazza, P.C., & M.M. Ostrosky. With M. Stalega, H-W. Yang, K. Aronson-Ensign, M. Block, W.C. Cheung, & Y. Akemoğlu. 2023. *CHAMPPS: CHildren in Action Motor Program for PreschoolerS*. Baltimore: Brookes.

Fox, L., G. Dunlap, & J. Ferro. 2021. "Implementing Individualized Behavior Support for Children with Persistent Challenging Behavior." In *Unpacking the Pyramid Model: A Practical Guide for Preschool Teachers*, eds. M.L. Hemmeter, M.M. Ostrosky, & L. Fox, 151–60. Baltimore: Brookes.

Fox, L., J. Carta, P. Strain, G. Dunlap, & M.L. Hemmeter. 2010. "Response to Intervention and the Pyramid Model." *Infants & Young Children* 23 (1): 3–13.

Fox, L., G. Dunlap, M.L. Hemmeter, G.E. Joseph, & P.S. Strain. 2003. "The Teaching Pyramid: A Model for Supporting Social Competence and Preventing Challenging Behavior in Young Children." *Young Children* 58 (4): 48–52.

Franzen, K., & D. Kamps. 2008. "The Utilization and Effects of Positive Behavior Support Strategies on an Urban School Playground." *Journal of Positive Behavior Interventions* 10 (3): 150–61.

Hemmeter, M.L., M.M. Ostrosky, & L. Fox. 2021. *Unpacking the Pyramid Model: A Practical Guide for Preschool Teachers.* Baltimore: Brookes.

Horn, E.M., S.B. Palmer, G.D. Butera, & J. Lieber. 2016. *Six Steps to Inclusive Preschool Curriculum: A UDL-Based Framework for Children's School Success.* Baltimore: Brookes.

Leedy, A., P. Bates, & S.P. Safran. 2004. "Bridging the Research-to-Practice Gap: Improving Hallway Behavior Using Positive Behavior Supports." *Behavioral Disorders* 29 (2): 130–39.

McNamara, L., Y. Lakman, N. Spadafora, K. Lodewyk, & M. Walker. 2018. "Recess and Children with Disabilities: A Mixed-Methods Pilot Study." *Disability and Health Journal* 11 (4): 637–43.

Meyer, L.E., M.E. Milan, & M.M. Ostrosky. 2021. "Friendship Skills and Strategies for Teaching Them." In *Unpacking the Pyramid Model: A Practical Guide for Preschool Teachers*, eds. M.L. Hemmeter, M.M. Ostrosky, & L. Fox, 109–18. Baltimore: Brookes.

Mulryan-Kyne, C. 2014. "The School Playground Experience: Opportunities and Challenges for Children and School Staff." *Educational Studies* 40 (4): 377–95.

NAECS-SDE (National Association of Early Childhood Specialists in State Departments of Education). 2001. "Recess and the Importance of Play: A Position Statement on Young Children and Recess." Position statement. Denver, CO: NAECS-SDE.

NAEYC. 2020. "Developmentally Appropriate Practice." Position statement. Washington, DC: NAEYC. www.naeyc.org/resources/position-statements/dap.

Piercy, K.L., & R.P. Troiano. 2018. "Physical Activity Guidelines for Americans from the US Department of Health and Human Services: Cardiovascular Benefits and Recommendations." *Circulation: Cardiovascular Quality and Outcomes* 11 (11): e005263.

Test, J.E., D.D. Cunningham, & A.C. Lee. 2010. "Talking with Young Children: How Teachers Encourage Learning." *Dimensions of Early Childhood* 38 (3): 3–14.

Todd, A., L. Haugen, K. Anderson, & M. Spriggs. 2002. "Teaching Recess: Low-Cost Efforts Producing Effective Results." *Journal of Positive Behavior Interventions* 4 (1): 46–52.

Westling, D.L. 2010. "Teachers and Challenging Behavior: Knowledge, Views, and Practices." *Remedial and Special Education* 31 (1): 48–63.

About the Authors

Hsiu-Wen Yang, PhD, is research investigator at the Frank Porter Graham Child Development Institute, University of North Carolina at Chapel Hill. Her research focuses on early intervention, family-centered practices, parent coaching, inclusive practices, and social and emotional development.

Michaelene M. Ostrosky, PhD, is Grayce Wicall Gauthier professor of education in the department of Special Education at the University of Illinois Urbana-Champaign. Throughout her career, she has been involved in research and dissemination of findings on the inclusion of children with disabilities, social and emotional competence, and challenging behavior.

Paddy Cronin Favazza, EdD, is senior research fellow at Saint Anselm College. As a special education professor, her research focuses on literacy-based strategies to support the acceptance of young children with disabilities and preschool curriculum for inclusive physical activities.

Yusuf Akemoğlu, PhD, is associate professor of early childhood special education at Duzce University in Turkey. His research focuses on behavior management and parent-implemented interventions for young children with autism spectrum disorder.

W. Catherine Cheung, PhD, PT, is assistant professor at the Doctor of Physical Therapy program at Northern Illinois University. Her research focuses on the impact of physical activity on the development of motor, cognitive, communication, and social skills on children with disabilities, including children with autism spectrum disorder.

Katherine Aronson-Ensign, PhD, is associate director of research and evaluation at Jumpstart for Young Children. She has worked on *CHAMPPS: CHildren in Action Motor Program for PreschoolerS*, a motor program for preschoolers with and without disabilities, inclusive education projects, and sports for development and peace research.

Targeted Practices

After implementing preventive supports for all children, there may be some children who require more targeted instruction focused on core social and emotional skills, such as self-regulation, friendship, problem solving, and effective communication. Many young children with specialized needs (e.g., disabilities, toxic stress exposure) require more intentional teaching and learning opportunities to develop these important skills in a nurturing and supportive environment.

The four articles in this part focus on explicit instruction of core aspects of social and emotional teaching.

In "Building Meaningful Relationships: Tips for Children Who Display Challenging Behavior," **Cecilia Scott-Croff** and **Sori Palacio** present a case study about a 4-year-old child who has experienced exclusionary discipline practices and struggles with regulating his emotions. The authors provide four targeted strategies that the child's teachers can implement to build connections and teach him more appropriate ways to regulate his emotions.

Kyla McRoy, Hope K. Gerde, and **Laurie Linscott** offer more strategies in their article, "A Three-Step Approach: Promoting Young Children's Self-Regulation and Language During Conflict." Children engage in challenging behavior because it is effective in communicating their needs. Teaching children more appropriate ways to communicate by bridging connections across language and feelings is a primary way to enhance their social and emotional understanding.

"Instead of Discipline, Use Guidance" provides a candid discussion of how to use guidance principles to shepherd children's development. **Dan Gartrell** offers a coaching approach that seeks to increase children's appropriate behavior and skills and decrease challenging behavior.

"Responses to Challenging Behavior: Why Some Common Strategies Don't Work and What to Do Instead" echoes similar sentiments and focuses on teaching skills and redirecting children by reinforcing desired behavior. **Keri Giordano, Emily Kokkinakis,** and **Briana Calcagno-Davi** highlight that it does not work to punish children, as this diminishes opportunities that could be focused on teaching or redirection and may further exacerbate social, emotional, and behavioral concerns. Instead, they emphasize addressing the reasons *why* children engage in certain behaviors and teaching them more appropriate ways to fulfill their needs.

Building Meaningful Relationships

Tips for Children Who Display Challenging Behavior

Cecilia Scott-Croff and Sori Palacio

Albert, who is 4 years old, often engages in disruptive behavior in his preschool classroom. He also finds it difficult to form relationships with his peers. His teachers have tried many conventional methods for guiding Albert toward more positive interactions and behaviors, but they have seen little progress and feel like they are failing him. Albert's mother does not have a strong relationship with his teachers and refuses to consent to testing to see if Albert would qualify for specialized services.

The director of Albert's preschool wants to continue to support him and his family while also supporting his teachers. She understands that his teachers feel they have done all they can; she also knows that Albert's mother has been scarred by her own experiences with special education and is not yet satisfied that his teachers have really tried to connect with him.

Recently, Albert's mother has begun to question the approaches his teachers are using. He's spending more and more time outside of the classroom—in the director's office or with the social worker. The teachers' frustrations have grown, and their demeanors are beginning to convey indifference toward Albert. Not surprisingly, Albert has reacted by engaging in even more kicking, spitting, running, and jumping throughout the classroom.

The director knows she needs to intervene. She blocks off time to spend in Albert's classroom; this will prevent his teachers from sending him out and will also allow her to see what methods they are using to try to guide him. She is open to more strongly encouraging Albert's mother to consider testing, but first she wants to know if his teachers are warmly, consistently, and supportively interacting with him.

Albert and everyone who cares for him are in a tough—but not unusual—situation. Many young children have social, emotional, and/or cognitive challenges that mean they need extra support to learn self-regulation and how to form positive relationships. Helping these children is an all-encompassing— and often overwhelming—undertaking.

Based on our combined 50 years of supporting children and our review of relevant research, we share four strategies for interacting with children in ways that promote their well-being and prosocial behavior.

Strategy 1: Ignore Unacceptable Behavior, but Don't Ignore the Child

Supporting the development of young children requires intentionality, reflection, and careful planning. You may feel like you have to respond every time a child behaves inappropriately; during these challenging moments, consider practicing *planned ignoring*: strategically ignoring unacceptable behavior and reinforcing acceptable behavior. Certainly, if a child is exhibiting behavior that could be dangerous to himself or others, you must intervene. But if there is no risk of injury, planned ignoring can be a proactive approach to deescalating situations. Intentionality is key, so ignoring the behavior does not mean ignoring the child. In fact, the child may be acting inappropriately to get your attention. Providing positive attention, especially for prosocial behavior, is a great way to attend to a child's needs.

Strategy 2: Remain Near the Child Who Is Experiencing a Challenge

Helping children manage strong feelings can benefit both the child and you. Responding calmly and consistently and staying close to a child in distress enables you to minimize the risk of injury while also giving the child a sense of belonging and worth when they see that an adult is caring and willing to help.

Applying appropriate, gentle touch to a child's back is often an effective way to create a connection, redirecting as well as reassuring the child. We encourage soft, caring touches unless the child has sensory integration issues or an aversion to being touched. For most children, light and reassuring touches help in relaxing their bodies and in building trust and connection with you.

Strategy 3: Acknowledge and Model Appropriate Behavior

A simple way you can increase children's acceptable behavior is to verbally acknowledge and commend it. Be specific, describing what the child is doing well (rather than using a vague comment such as "good job"). Also, try to model appropriate ways to handle frustrations, stress, and disappointment, including helping children find appropriate outlets for strong emotions.

Even when they are in distress, children can read adults' frustrations in their voices and body language. It's hard, but you should strive to support a child who is acting out as calmly and warmly as possible. When you respond calmly, it helps demonstrate that you care, which then helps the child feel protected and appreciated. Soon, the child will likely see you as a trusted adult and may become more open about what is causing her distress and inappropriate behavior.

Strategy 4: Adapt the Environment

For children who are slowly learning to self-regulate, a classroom that is crowded with interesting activities may invite problems with impulse control. If possible, consider having fewer activities in the classroom each day and rotating activities out of and into the classroom more often. This way, children can still experience an array of activities, but they won't have an overwhelming number of choices (or temptations!) on any one day.

To enable all children to safely participate in activities, think about what modifications you could make. For example, if a child often throws balls inside the classroom, consider setting up a ramp and ball area with foam balls instead of wooden ones. While the throwing behavior still needs to be addressed, engaging the child in the activity is also a priority. Experimenting with balls and ramps provides an introduction to physics—and doing so with peers offers opportunities to learn from classmates' examples of prosocial behavior.

Building a Relationship with Albert

With the director's support, Albert's teachers used these four strategies consistently. They started to see progress in a few weeks and achieved meaningful changes in his behavior after a few months. Although initially skeptical, Albert's mother soon realized that their efforts were genuine. She was deeply appreciative and began using the same four strategies at home. Like so many children, warmth, consistency, and intentional supports (like offering interesting yet limited choices) were what Albert needed to calm down and begin to self-regulate.

While these four strategies were what worked best with Albert, some additional strategies also helped. For example, Albert found it comforting to keep a drawing of his mother with him, especially on his tough days. Albert's behavior also improved when he felt that he was contributing to his classroom community.

Big Feelings: Children's Books for Dealing with Strong Emotions

Engaging children in carefully selected picture books is a tried and true strategy for learning about and dealing with emotions. Here are some of our favorite books for reading aloud and for tucking into cozy corners:

> *Calm-Down Time/Momento para calmarse,* by Elizabeth Verdick

> *Cool Down and Work Through Anger,* by Cheri J. Meiners

> *F Is for Feelings,* by Goldie Millar and Lisa A. Berger

> *Happy Hippo, Angry Duck: A Book of Moods,* by Sandra Boynton

> *How to Take the Grrrr Out of Anger,* by Elizabeth Verdick and Marjorie Lisovskis

Reflection Questions

1. What are some steps you can take to connect with children and their families early in the relationship (before conflicts arise)?

2. If you have a strong relationship with a child, how does that change or impact how you respond to the challenging behavior?

3. Reflect on who in the school or community might have a strong relationship with a family of a child with challenging behavior. How might you leverage their support to connect with the child's family?

He liked taking on roles such as selecting books for read alouds, setting up and cleaning up activities, and taking papers to the copier for a teacher. As they tuned into Albert's strengths and needs, his teachers learned to use these roles when he seemed like he needed a break. A short walk to the copy room and back could defuse an interaction with another child and also reminded Albert of how valuable he was to his teachers as a helper.

Creating a classroom that supports divergent strategies—including creative approaches to redirecting behavior—leads to greater inclusivity. Just as important, seeing the benefits of diverse approaches helps us reconsider how we think and feel about challenging behavior. Albert's teachers and mother were not the only ones being challenged—Albert was too. Realizing this, his teachers reframed their efforts toward creating a safe space for all and building a new relationship with a child who needed their support.

About the Authors

Cecilia Scott-Croff, EdD, SAS, SDA, CPAC, has more than 30 years of experience in the fields of early childhood, special education, and advocacy. Cecilia serves as the executive director of the Early Childhood Center at Borough of Manhattan Community College. She is governing board president of the New York Association for the Education of Young Children and a proud mom.

Sori Palacio has over 20 years of experience working with preschool children and their families. She has served as a teacher and adjunct professor in the department of Early Childhood Education at the Borough of Manhattan Community College.

Photographs: pp. 58, 59, 60, 61 © Getty Images

A Three-Step Approach

Promoting Young Children's Self-Regulation and Language During Conflict

Kyla McRoy, Hope K. Gerde, and Laurie Linscott

It is work time in the Riverbend Room, and preschoolers Jamaya and Ian are playing in the block area. Ian picks up a block from the floor beside him to add to his zoo enclosure, but Jamaya wants the same block for her airport. She shrieks and reaches to grab it. Ian jerks it away. Both children begin to shout.

The teacher, Ms. Williams, runs over. This is the third time this week that disagreements between Jamaya and Ian have erupted into a shouting match, and Ms. Williams is running out of ideas to calm these situations. The rest of the class looks on as she approaches the two.

A comprehensive early childhood curriculum includes practices to promote development and learning in all domains (NAEYC 2020). In that context, early childhood educators recognize that the development of self-regulation goes hand-in-hand with growth in other areas, such as language. This article presents a three-step approach to address common behavioral challenges and social conflicts in early childhood classrooms while simultaneously promoting children's self-regulation and language development. The approach uses a *personal message*, or a way "to express expectations and rules for children's behavior . . . to give children the information they need for both current and future reference" (Kostelnik et al. 2006, 337–38). It was developed by researchers and educators at Michigan State University (Kostelnik et al. 2019; also see Meece & Soderman 2010 for guidance). The use of personal messages remains at the heart of the university's teacher preparation program due to its foundation in existing research and its positive outcomes for preservice educators and children alike. Although this article focuses on preschool, the approach can be adapted for children birth to grade 3.

The Importance of Self-Regulation

Self-regulation develops over time and encompasses multiple skills. These include inhibitory control, working memory, and cognitive flexibility (McClelland et al. 2014). (See "Self-Regulatory Skills" on page 65 for definitions of these and examples of how children demonstrate them through their behaviors and words.) Effective teachers create positive learning environments by helping children learn to regulate their behavior and emotions. They do this by

> Establishing expectations for behavior ("We are kind," "We touch books gently")

> Defining and discussing prosocial or helping behaviors ("How can we help Dominic solve his problem?," "How can we both use the trucks?")

> Modeling the behaviors they want to see

> Describing children's positive behavior when it is observed

Yet even with well-established behavior expectations, at times young children still engage in unsafe behavior and experience conflicts. Many teachers, such as Ms. Williams, are unsure how to help them resolve these situations.

Early childhood is a critical time to support self-regulation because children develop these skills rapidly between ages 3 and 7 (Montroy et al. 2016). Children with higher self-regulation skills experience more positive peer relationships (Robson, Allen, & Howard 2020) than those still developing them. They also are better able to actively engage in classroom learning opportunities (Montroy et al. 2016). This is not surprising—when children can keep rules and instructions in mind, concentrate on their work, and transition between tasks effectively, they can focus more on learning-related interactions and activities. Indeed, research shows that children with higher self-regulation have higher academic achievement in preschool and elementary grades (Ursache, Blair, & Raver 2012).

Self-Regulation and Language Development

A child's self-regulation is influenced by developmental processes that occur emotionally, cognitively, and linguistically (Kostelnik et al. 2019). At the same time, self-regulation plays a vital role in supporting children's development in these domains. With language specifically, self-regulation promotes children's ability to engage in language-learning experiences: children with higher self-regulation skills tend to participate in classroom activities more regularly and show greater gains in language across the preschool year (Bohlmann & Downer 2016). Self-regulation may also promote language development as children interact socially with one another (e.g., Skibbe et al. 2019).

Yet because self-regulation and language skills continue to develop throughout early childhood (Bohlmann, Maier, & Palacios 2015), even elementary-age children may find it difficult to manage their behaviors and use appropriate strategies for effective communication. As such, unsafe behaviors or conflicts may arise due to children's emerging self-regulation and language skills.

Early childhood educators play an essential role in children's development of these skills. When teachers target self-regulation and language during classroom interactions and conflicts, children become more capable of using the upcoming strategies to interact with peers and problem solve appropriately (Pidano & Allen 2015). By following the steps outlined below, teachers can effectively support both children's self-regulation and language development while addressing unsafe, destructive, or conflict-related behaviors in the classroom.

Self-Regulatory Skills

Children use self-regulation when they follow directions, remember rules and procedures, persist in a task, or adjust to a change. Definitions of the three types of self-regulatory skills follow, along with ways that children demonstrate them.

> **Inhibitory control** is the ability to resist instinctive urges in favor of more socially appropriate behaviors. Children demonstrate inhibitory control when they pick up toys after the clean-up song plays rather than continuing to play, or when they ask to take turns instead of snatching another child's toy.

> **Working memory** is how children manage and store information short-term for use in their play and learning. Children demonstrate working memory when they remember classroom rules, the four steps to washing their hands, or the rules for playing a game.

> **Cognitive flexibility** is the ability to adapt to changing rules or information. A child exercises this skill when

  • They are immersed in outside play, clean-up is announced, and they must stop their play to clean up and return to the classroom

  • They want to play in the block area but choose another activity when they see that there is no space

The Three-Step Approach to Promoting Self-Regulation and Language During Conflict

Research has documented different styles or approaches for adults thinking about and responding to children's behavior (although that research has traditionally been associated with parenting and Western cultural conceptions). These include authoritarian, permissive, authoritative, and uninvolved (or rejecting/neglecting) (Kuppens & Ceulemans 2019; Smetana 2017). Some have extended these styles to describe classroom management or guidance approaches by educators (Omdal 2018).

The steps presented here align with the authoritative discipline approach. In both home and classroom settings, an authoritative approach is characterized by adults creating nurturing and communicative relationships with children, using positive guidance, fostering independence, and providing high levels of structure. An authoritative discipline style is strongly associated with self-regulation development in children (Piotrowski, Lapierre, & Linebarger 2013). Beyond more global discipline styles, recent research has revealed that it can be especially valuable to focus on specific practices (Spinrad, Morris, & Luthar 2020), like the approach discussed here.

Following, we outline the steps an effective early childhood educator can use to help children resolve conflicts while promoting self-regulation and language. ("Applying the Three-Step Approach in Early Childhood Classrooms" on page 69 includes additional scenarios.) While these steps represent a progression, it is important to remember that children's behavior is rarely linear. Thus, it may be necessary to cycle through the three steps multiple times before an issue is resolved. This is especially true for more intense emotional conflicts (Wiltshire 2018).

Step One: State the Behavior and Help Identify Emotions

Just as teachers can acknowledge children's positive behavior in the classroom, they can also describe behavior that is not appropriate. Clearly and briefly describing children's behavior draws their attention to their actions (Malott 2016) and gives them the language they need for future discussions or interactions. For example, if a child is shoveling sand onto the floor at the sensory area, a teacher might say, "Micah, you are pouring sand out of the sensory table onto the floor." This makes the child aware of their behavior and sets the stage for the teacher to explain and address it (steps two and three).

This first step is also an excellent opportunity for teachers to use emotion vocabulary to help children understand and label the feelings that might be related to their behavior (Nix et al. 2013). Research shows that supporting children in labeling and discussing their emotions can promote their self-regulation development (Silkenbeumer, Schiller, & Kärtner 2018). This is likely because it provides children with the language to accurately identify and express their feelings when conflicts arise. When teachers acknowledge children's feelings, they help children feel heard and set the stage for a compassionate discussion rather than a power struggle. For very young children, teachers may use basic emotion language (*happy, sad, angry*) to support children's early understanding. As children develop, teachers can expand children's language by using richer or more complex emotion vocabulary, such as *gloomy, frustrated, anxious,* or *discouraged.*

Examples of Rich Emotion Vocabulary

Emotion vocabulary can help children understand and label their feelings. While teachers may use basic language to support very young children's understanding of emotions, they can move to richer, more complex vocabulary as children develop their language skills.

Basic emotion vocabulary	sad	angry	happy	other
More complex vocabulary	gloomy troubled distressed miserable sorrowful discouraged lonely glum	flustered annoyed frustrated irritated furious cross enraged grumpy	enthusiastic pleased eager thrilled proud elated interested delighted	anxious startled puzzled impatient amused shocked restless disgusted

For example, a 3-year-old struggling to balance blocks on a tower might yell, causing a teacher to kneel beside them and say, "You are yelling. It sounds like you are *angry*." An older child may grab materials or climb onto a table, which would prompt a teacher to say, "You are climbing on the table. You seem *eager* to start." (See "Examples of Rich Emotion Vocabulary" on page 66 for more emotion-rich words.)

Though teachers can suggest these emotion labels based on what children appear to be feeling, it is important to remember that this is just a guess. Children may be feeling a different emotion, which teachers can help them identify. For example, a child might appear upset about accidentally ripping their easel paper while painting, to which the teacher can respond, "You are kicking the easel. I am wondering if you are *frustrated*?" If the child does not answer or says, "I don't know," the teacher can then say, "It seems like you might be frustrated about your paper tearing. Is that right?" The child may confirm or deny this emotion label, and the teacher can make further suggestions or ask the child what label they would use.

A feelings chart can help children label and discuss emotions. The National Center for Pyramid Model Innovations offers an example at www.challengingbehavior.org/docs/ FeelingFaces_chart_template.pdf. For older children, teachers may begin by asking "How are you feeling?" or "Tell me what happened" to understand the child's perspective.

Special considerations may be present in this first step because conflicts can vary in intensity and may not always require a teacher's direct involvement. "When Should I Intervene?" offers additional guidance on this point.

When Should I Intervene?

Some behaviors—such as unsafe or destructive actions or intense social conflicts—signal an immediate need for teacher intervention. These could include

> A child knocking classroom plants off the windowsill

> Two children shouting and pulling on either end of the classroom headphones

> A child climbing onto the bookshelf and jumping off

In these cases, teachers should approach the children involved calmly and stop any dangerous or hurtful actions (Kostelnik et al. 2018) before labeling the behavior. If an object is involved, the teacher can neutralize the item by holding onto it while the issue is discussed.

In other social conflicts, teachers may not need to intervene immediately, but rather observe and stay nearby. These include situations in which

> Children are actively working through the issue, and their behavior is not escalating

> One or more of the children involved are more skilled at communicating and resolving conflicts

> The teacher has recently discussed conflict resolution strategies with children

In any of these scenarios, children may benefit from the opportunity to work through an issue without teacher intervention.

Step Two: Explain the Behavior and Its Implications

After teachers have drawn children's attention to their behaviors and helped them identify their emotions, they can explain the reasons why that behavior may be inappropriate. When adults model the use of reasoning, children tend to have better self-regulation skills and reduced aggression than children who do not have these models (Akçinar 2013). They also begin to recognize cause and effect (Perret 2015), which supports their future ability to use reasoning to regulate their behavior without teacher support. (See "What About Consequences?" on this page for a discussion of reasoning versus teacher-imposed repercussions.)

Step two is also a great opportunity for teachers to refer back to the behavioral expectations they have already established with children. Providing children with a reason that reflects classroom rules or speaks to children's personal interests can reinforce their internalization of rules and help motivate them to adjust their behaviors (Denno, Carr, & Bell 2011). For example, if a child is dumping toy cars all over the floor, the teacher could say, "You are dumping the cars all over the floor. You seem so excited to play. Children may step on the cars and fall and hurt themselves, or their feet might break the cars so we cannot use them anymore." Another child might throw a book, causing it to tear and prompting the teacher to say, "You tore this book. We will not be able to read it. Remember that one of our classroom rules is to take care of our books. Be gentle with our books."

Teachers can also take this opportunity to support children's language more broadly by using rich vocabulary. For example, if a child is working on their picture as the class starts to transition, the teacher can say, "You are still *illustrating* the story you wrote. If you keep working on your *illustration* right now, you will miss free play time."

What About Consequences?

Traditional methods of addressing challenging behavior have often emphasized teacher-implemented consequences, such as time-outs (isolation) or deducting "points" from children (using clip/behavior charts). Recent research shows that these kinds of consequences are not appropriate or beneficial for children's development (e.g., Kowalski & Froiland 2020). Punitive consequences can

> Fail to teach children what they could have done instead

> Risk emotional harm (fear, shame, embarrassment, stress, rejection), which can lead to future problems

> Teach children to distrust, manipulate, or lie to teachers

> Build reliance on external sources of motivation and regulation (e.g., pleasing the teacher to avoid punishment) rather than motivating internal self-regulation

Step Three: Address the Behavior

Now that children are aware of their actions and the related implications, teachers can guide children's behavior by providing an alternative, appropriate behavior. This gives children an action they can pursue instead, which supports their ability to disengage from the inappropriate one (Shelleby et al. 2012). In the following example, a child is attempting to use scissors to cut their clothing. Step three is underlined.

Teacher: (*Stops the child's hands gently.*) You are using the scissors to cut your shirt. You seem curious about how scissors work. Is that right?

Child: I am cutting.

Teacher: Yes, you are cutting your shirt with the scissors. The scissors may ruin your clothes or hurt you. <u>Use the scissors to cut your construction paper, or choose another item from the art center like the felt strips. Which will you choose?</u>

Applying the Three-Step Approach in Early Childhood Classrooms

Scenario	Step 1: State the Behavior	Step 2: Explain the Behavior	Step 3: Address the Behavior
A child is spilling water during a sink-float activity.	"You are spilling the water onto the floor. You seem curious about it."	"If the floor is wet, children may slip and fall."	"Keep the water in the tub, and use this paper towel to dry the floor."
Two children both want to use the toy cell phone.	"You are pushing and grabbing. I am thinking that you both want to use the phone."	"I am worried that you may hurt yourselves by pushing or break the phone when you grab."	"What can we do to solve this problem?"
A child is bothering their peer during large group.	"You are talking very loudly to Keely. It seems like you are very excited to share a story."	"I cannot hear other children when you are talking loudly."	"You can use the clipboard to write quietly about your story while Jeremy is telling us about the weather."
A wheel has broken off a child's truck.	"You are screaming and kicking the truck. You sound so upset."	"Your screaming is hurting my ears and other children's ears, and I am concerned that if you kick the truck, we will not be able to fix it."	"Let's work together to brainstorm ways to fix the truck. How do you think we can put the wheel back on?"
A child is refusing to clean up after free choice.	"It looks like you are distressed about cleaning up. You are lying on the floor."	"We need to put our toys away so they will be safe and we can learn our new song at large group."	"Will you pick up the blocks or the animals first?"
Children walking through the block area are knocking over others' projects.	"I am hearing alarmed and flustered voices from children in the block area."	"I see that other children are walking through the block area, and their feet are damaging several projects."	"Today at large group, we will all generate ideas to address this problem."

Sometimes children benefit when teachers provide a solution ("Soil stays in the flowerbed"). This language is useful when a simple, brief reminder suffices, based on the teacher's knowledge of the child or situation.

In other instances, giving children a few replacement choices can be effective (Cadima et al. 2019). This is especially true in cases involving heightened emotions, such as when children feel particularly attached to their current inappropriate behavior or when they struggle to engage in an expected behavior, as in the following example.

Teacher: You are throwing your jacket and mittens. What is going on?

Child: I don't want to.

Teacher: You seem frustrated about getting ready to go outside. It can be a hassle to put on our snow clothes.

Child: I am not frustrated.

Teacher: You are not frustrated? Okay. I am thinking you may be overwhelmed or distracted then? There is a lot going on in the classroom when all the children are putting on their snow clothes.

Child: Yeah, it is a lot!

Teacher: I know! It is cold outside, so you must wear snow clothes to go outdoors. You will miss outside time if you do not put on your outdoor clothes. Will you put on your coat or your hat first?

Effective teachers can stimulate children's language use during this step by helping them identify what to say during a conflict. Depending on the child's language skills, teachers may need to

> Provide the language for resolving a conflict ("Tiana, did you want to help Sam with the puzzle? You can say, 'Sam, can I help?'")

> Offer choices about what to say ("Do you want to ask Gayle to 'Please pass the water pitcher' or do you want to ask Marco?")

> Prompt children to think about what they could say independently ("Violet, what could you say to Akshay if you want to take a turn?")

Teachers can powerfully target both self-regulation and language during this step by supporting children to brainstorm alternative behaviors or solutions (Wiltshire 2018). Questions such as "What solutions can you generate to fix this problem?" or "How can we resolve this issue?" prompt children to pause their behavior while they analyze the situation and discuss potential solutions.

This is an advanced skill for children, and it requires teacher guidance for success, especially since children often struggle to communicate and engage in problem solving when they are upset. Effective teachers can support children first to calm down, then to verbalize their current problem and think through the challenge. They can restate children's ideas to acknowledge them and check their appeal to other children (Evans 2016). If children struggle to come up with their own solutions, teachers may provide additional support by saying, "I have an idea. Would you like to hear my idea?" After several consistent iterations with teacher support, children will gradually take on more responsibilities or steps to address problems more independently, thus truly learning to *self*-regulate.

Once children have agreed upon a solution, they can implement it independently or with teacher support (Pidano & Allen 2015). Educators should remember that solutions viewed positively by the children involved are ideal—even if they do not seem fair from an adult's perspective. They also must remember that conflict may arise again. Teachers should remain nearby to ensure that children do not need to revisit certain steps. If they do, teachers can help them cycle back through each step and apply it to the new conflict—again supporting them to use their language.

The National Center for Pyramid Model Innovations offers a visual guide that can help children through their problem-solving steps (www.challengingbehavior.org/docs/SocialEmotionalSkills_problem-solving-steps_wrist.pdf). Children can also create their own problem-solving plans, which they can refer to when conflicts arise. For example, if two children are arguing over a toy, the teacher can say, "Let's review your play plans and see who planned to play with the fire truck today."

The Three Steps in Action

Now let's return to the opening vignette and see these three steps in action.

As Ian and Jamaya argue over the blocks, Ms. Williams calmly approaches them. She begins at step one, saying, "Ian and Jamaya, you are yelling and trying to grab each other's blocks. You seem furious." She gently stops their hands. "I will hold onto this block while we find a solution."

Keeping the desired block where both children can see it, Ms. Williams then proceeds to step two. "Your yelling hurts other children's ears and my ears, and you might hurt each other when you hit." With this statement, both children are reminded how their behavior might upset others and cause pain to themselves.

"How should we solve this problem?" Ms. Williams asks, moving to step three.

"We can use a timer," says Ian. Ms. Williams replies, "You are thinking you could use a timer to take turns using the block. What do you think, Jamaya?"

Jamaya frowns and says, "No." Ms. Williams nods thoughtfully and says, "Hmmm. It does not sound like that idea works for Jamaya. Jamaya, do you have a different idea?"

Jamaya points to another block in Ian's pile and says, "I want that one. I give you this one." Ms. Williams turns to Ian and says, "Ian, it sounds like Jamaya is willing to trade her block—this one that I am holding—for one of your blocks. Does that idea work for you?" Ian nods, and Ms. Williams says, "Okay, so Ian will take this block, and Jamaya will take that block. Did we solve the problem?" Both children agree and take their respective blocks. Ms. Williams adds, "We were respectful to each other when we solved that problem, just like our classroom rule says!"

For Further Resources

Want to learn more? The following resources are free and valuable for teachers and families looking for additional ways to implement the three-step approach.

> **National Center for Pyramid Model Innovations**
> This site offers practice briefs, roadmaps to effective intervention practices, videos, webinars, fact sheets, posters, and articles, all largely focused on addressing challenging behavior. (www.challengingbehavior.org/resources)

> **Head Start Early Childhood Learning & Knowledge Center**
> This resource offers effective practice guides for emotional and behavioral self-regulation. These are broken into sections titled "Know," "See," "Do," and "Improve"—each with text and videos. (https://eclkc.ohs.acf.hhs.gov/school-readiness/effective-practice-guides/emotional-behavioral-self-regulation)

> **HighScope Conflict Resolution Videos**
> These videos show teachers applying conflict-resolution strategies in real preschool classrooms. (www.youtube.com/watch?v=nXMSKxlfW28&list=PL2prU6Y0rzH6uzywtweGe3RXZguPEKqnu&pp=iAQB)

> "Preschool: Promoting Young Children's Social and Emotional Health," by Jeannie Ho and Suzanne Funk, in the March 2018 issue of *Young Children*.

Reflection Questions

1. How do you model appropriate self-regulation for young children?

2. How can you increase your self-awareness of what you are communicating to children when using the three-step approach (state the behavior, explain the behavior, address the behavior)?

3. How might you help children describe their emotions and expand their emotion vocabularies to facilitate their self-regulation and conflict resolution efforts?

4. How might predictable routines and transitions support self-regulation skills?

Conclusion

The early development of self-regulation and language is critical for children's success in both school and life. Teachers play a valuable role in supporting these skills during unsafe or conflict-related behavior. By using the three-step approach to state the behavior, explain the implications of the behavior, and address the behavior, effective teachers support self-regulation and language simultaneously. Importantly, these three steps can be easily adapted by teachers to suit children's ages, abilities, interests, and ideas.

It is important to understand that adopting this approach and making it second nature take practice. Teachers should not expect to master the three-step approach overnight, but they can support the development of these skills by posting reminders and prompts around the classroom to refer to—especially in areas where conflicts tend to occur more often because of increased social interactions (like in the block or dramatic play areas).

It is also important to remember that certain heated situations may cause teachers to feel stressed or upset themselves. In these cases, they should take a moment to self-regulate and calm themselves before approaching their children. This may require taking a couple of deep breaths or mentally reframing the conflict as an opportunity to engage children in developing self-regulatory and language skills. A supportive mantra, such as "The children are not giving me a hard time; they are having a hard time," may help. Teachers can also work to view themselves as a mediator, or a wise but neutral guide whose purpose is to help each child on the path to self-regulation and effective communication.

REFERENCES

Akçinar, B. 2013. "The Predictors of School Adaptation in Early Childhood." *Procedia–Social and Behavioral Sciences* 93: 1099–104.

Bohlmann, N.L., & J.T. Downer. 2016. "Self-Regulation and Task Engagement as Predictors of Emergent Language and Literacy Skills." *Early Education and Development* 27 (1): 18–37.

Bohlmann, N.L., M.F. Maier, & N. Palacios. 2015. "Bidirectionality in Self-Regulation and Expressive Vocabulary: Comparisons Between Monolingual and Dual Language Learners in Preschool." *Child Development* 86 (4): 1094–111.

Cadima, J., S. Barros, T. Ferreira, M. Serra-Lemos, T. Leal, & K. Verschueren. 2019. "Bidirectional Associations Between Vocabulary and Self-Regulation in Preschool and Their Interplay with Teacher-Child Closeness and Autonomy Support." *Early Childhood Research Quarterly* 46: 75–86.

Denno, D.M., V. Carr, & S.H. Bell. 2011. *Addressing Challenging Behaviors in Early Childhood Settings: A Teacher's Guide*. Baltimore: Brookes.

Evans, B. 2016. *You Can't Come to My Birthday Party! Conflict Resolution with Young Children*. 2nd ed. Ypsilanti, MI: HighScope Press.

Kostelnik, M., A. Whiren, A. Soderman, & K. Gregory. 2006. *Guiding Children's Social Development Theory to Practice*. 5th ed. Clifton Park, NY: Thomson Delmar Learning.

Kostelnik, M., A. Whiren, A. Soderman, & M.L. Rupiper. 2018. *Guiding Children's Social Development and Learning*. 8th ed. Boston: Cengage Learning.

Kostelnik, M., A. Soderman,, A. Whiren, & M.L. Rupiper. 2019. *Guiding Children's Social Development and Learning*. 9th ed. Boston: Cengage Learning.

Kowalski, M.J., & J.M. Froiland. 2020. "Parent Perceptions of Elementary Classroom Management Systems and Their Children's Motivational and Emotional Responses." *Social Psychology of Education* 23 (2): 433–48.

Kuppens, S., & E. Ceulemans. 2019. "Parenting Styles: A Closer Look at a Well-Known Concept." *Journal of Child and Family Studies* 28 (1): 168–81.

Malott, R. 2016. *Principles of Behavior.* 7th ed. Upper Saddle River, NJ: Routledge.

McClelland, M.M., C.E. Cameron, R. Duncan, R.P. Bowles, A.C. Acock, A. Miao, & M.E. Pratt. 2014. "Predictors of Early Growth in Academic Achievement: The Head-Toes-Knees-Shoulders Task." *Frontiers in Psychology* 5: 1–14.

Meece, D., & A. Soderman. 2010. "Positive Verbal Environments: Setting the Stage for Young Children's Social Development." *Young Children* 65 (5): 81–86.

Montroy, J.J., R.P. Bowles, L.E. Skibbe, M.M. McClelland, & F.J. Morrison. 2016. "The Development of Self-Regulation Across Early Childhood." *Developmental Psychology* 52 (11): 1744–62.

NAEYC. 2020. "Developmentally Appropriate Practice." Position statement. Washington, DC: NAEYC. www.naeyc.org/resources/position-statements/dap/contents.

Nix, R.L., K.L. Bierman, C.E. Domitrovich, & S. Gill. 2013. "Promoting Children's Social-Emotional Skills in Preschool Can Enhance Academic and Behavioral Functioning in Kindergarten: Findings from Head Start REDI." *Early Education & Development* 24 (7): 1000–19.

Omdal, H. 2018. "Creating Teacher Capacity in Early Childhood Education and Care Institutions Implementing an Authoritative Adult Style." *Journal of Educational Change* 19 (1): 103–29.

Perret, P. 2015. "Children's Inductive Reasoning: Developmental and Educational Perspectives." *Journal of Cognitive Education and Psychology* 14 (3): 389–408.

Pidano, A.E., & A.R. Allen. 2015. "The Incredible Years Series: A Review of the Independent Research Base." *Journal of Child and Family Studies* 24 (7): 1898–916.

Piotrowski, J.T., M.A. Lapierre, & D.L. Linebarger. 2013. "Investigating Correlates of Self-Regulation in Early Childhood with a Representative Sample of English-Speaking American Families." *Journal of Child and Family Studies* 22 (3): 423–36.

Robson, D.A., M.S. Allen, & S.J. Howard. 2020. "Self-Regulation in Childhood as a Predictor of Future Outcomes: A Meta-Analytic Review." *Psychological Bulletin* 146 (4): 324.

Shelleby, E.C., D.S. Shaw, J. Cheong, H. Chang, F. Gardner, T.J. Dishion, & M.N. Wilson. 2012. "Behavioral Control in At-Risk Toddlers: The Influence of the Family Check-Up." *Journal of Clinical Child & Adolescent Psychology* 41 (3): 288–301.

Skibbe, L.E., J.J. Montroy, R.P. Bowles, & F.J. Morrison. 2019. "Self-Regulation and the Development of Literacy and Language Achievement from Preschool Through Second Grade." *Early Childhood Research Quarterly* 46: 240–51.

Silkenbeumer, J.R., E.-M. Schiller, & J. Kärtner. 2018. "Co- and Self-Regulation of Emotions in the Preschool Setting." *Early Childhood Research Quarterly* 44: 72–81.

Smetana, J.G. 2017. "Current Research on Parenting Styles, Dimensions, and Beliefs." *Current Opinion in Psychology* 15: 19–25.

Spinrad, T.L., A.S. Morris, & S.S. Luthar. 2020. "Introduction to the Special Issue: Socialization of Emotion and Self-Regulation: Understanding Processes and Application." *Developmental Psychology* 56 (3): 385.

Ursache, A., C. Blair, & C.C. Raver. 2012. "The Promotion of Self-Regulation as a Means of Enhancing School Readiness and Early Achievement in Children at Risk for School Failure." *Child Development Perspectives* 6 (2): 122–28.

Wiltshire, M. 2018. *Understanding the HighScope Approach: Early Years Education in Practice.* 2nd ed. New York: Routledge.

About the Authors

Kyla McRoy, MS, is a doctoral candidate in the department of Human Development and Family Studies at Michigan State University (MSU). Kyla has taught preservice and in-service teachers and worked as a preschool teacher at the MSU Child Development Laboratories. Her research focuses on developing effective strategies for supporting young children's self-regulation.

Hope K. Gerde, PhD, is professor and dean's excellence chair in the department of Teaching, Learning, and Culture at Texas A&M University. A former preschool teacher, her research focuses on the design of effective approaches to supporting the language and literacy development of young children.

Laurie Linscott, MA, is director of the MSU Child Development Laboratories. The two lab sites are accredited by NAEYC. Laurie's professional work focuses on preservice teacher training, inclusion, and community collaborations.

Instead of Discipline, Use Guidance

Dan Gartrell

We all know that we shouldn't punish young children when they exhibit challenging behavior. The children in our preschool classrooms are just beginning to learn the complex skills of getting along with others. These are skills that we humans work on our entire lives.

Children are going to have disagreements—sometimes dramatic ones—as they interact with others. They really don't "know better" because they haven't learned the "better" yet. After all, a 4-year-old has only 48 months of on-the-ground experience! It's our job to teach children positive lessons from their mistakes—and to make sure we don't hold their mistakes against them.

Conventional discipline too easily slides into punishment. For example, if we embarrass children by singling them out as part of our discipline strategy, this is punishment. Punishment makes young children feel stressed, hurt, rejected, and angry; these feelings make it harder for children to learn emotional and social skills.

When we punish children, we are actually making life more difficult for

> The child, who feels rejected and unworthy and becomes more challenged in learning social skills

> Other children, who worry for themselves and the punished child

> Adults, who are not being the leaders they want to be

Using Guidance

Guidance is about building an encouraging setting for every person in the group. It means helping young children understand they can learn from their mistakes, and it starts with showing them how. To give this help successfully, we need to build relationships with every child—especially with the children we find difficult to connect with and understand. We build these relationships from day one, outside of conflict situations. It is only when children know and trust us in day-to-day interactions that they will listen to us when conflicts happen (after we have helped everyone calm down).

So what do you do when conflicts arise and you want to use guidance? This article gives two illustrations of guidance at work. The first one might surprise you.

Illustration 1: Jeremiah Comes Through

This example comes from former preschool teacher Beth Wallace.

> When I first started working with Jeremiah, he had a lot of angry outbursts. The center used time-out at that point (the dreaded "green chair"), and Jeremiah spent considerable time there. While I was at the center, we moved away from using time-outs and introduced a system called peer problem solving. By the time Jeremiah graduated to kindergarten, we had been using the system for three years, and he was one of the experts.

> One day, I overheard a fracas in the block corner. I stood up to see what was going on, ready to intervene. Jordan, just 26 months old and only talking a little bit, had a truck. Franklin, 50 months old, decided it was his turn to use the truck. I took a step forward, ready to go to their aid, but paused when I saw Jeremiah (then 60 months old) approach them.

> "What's going on, guys?" Jeremiah asked (my standard opening line). He then facilitated a five-minute discussion between the two children. He made sure both got a chance to speak, interpreting for the little one. "Jordan, what do you think of that idea?" he asked. Jordan shook his head and clutched the truck tighter. "I don't think Jordan's ready to give up the truck yet," Jeremiah told Franklin.

> After helping his classmates negotiate an agreement, Jeremiah's competence was without question, and his pride was evident.

On this day, Beth knew that three years of building relationships and teaching children how to resolve their conflicts through mediation was paying off.

Illustration 2: Playdough Politics

In preschool, three common sources of conflicts are property, territory, and privilege. The following illustration is a combination of dozens of property-related conflicts I have worked with teachers to address. I put a magnifying glass to this one so you can see up close what guidance is and isn't, and how it teaches young children to learn from mistaken behavior.

Jason, age 42 months, is the only one at the playdough table. He gets a grin on his face and pulls the whole chunk of dough in front of him. He starts working the dough and mutters, "Makin' a dinosaur nest and eggs."

Daeisha, age 52 months, sits at the table and sees Jason has all the dough. She says, "Hey, give me some!" Jason hands Daeisha a tiny bit and circles his arms around the big mound. Daeisha responds by grabbing a large handful of dough out from under Jason's arm. Jason screams. When he tries to grab the dough back, Daeisha pushes him and starts kneading the playdough. Teacher Kris sees Jason on the floor, yowling, and Daeisha using playdough as if nothing has happened.

Pause for a few minutes to think about how you would address this situation. Then read on to consider two possible intervention choices.

Conventional discipline: Kris walks over to Daeisha, stands above her, and says loudly, "You've taken something from another person again, Daeisha. You need to sit on the time-out chair so you will remember how to share." Kris takes Daeisha to the chair.

Daeisha is *not* thinking, "I am glad the teacher has temporarily prevented me from playing. Now I will be a better child and use friendly words instead of forcing my will on others." Instead, Daeisha is embarrassed, hurt, and angry. She feels rejected by Kris and unwelcome in the group. Daeisha *is* thinking how to get back at Jason.

Guidance: Kris moves between the two children, kneels down, and takes the following five firm, friendly actions. Kris

1. **Describes** the scene. "I see Jason on the floor very upset. I see Daeisha using a big bunch of playdough. We need to solve this problem."

2. **Calms** who needs calming. "Jason, we need to help you cool down so we can make this better. Let's get you back on the chair." Taking the playdough, Kris looks at Daeisha and says to both children, "I will hold the playdough. Take some deep breaths or just close your eyes to get calm."

3. **Leads** each child to describe the conflict, often starting with the younger child.

    Kris: Jason, what do you think happened?

    Jason: I was making a dinosaur nest and Daeisha took my playdough!

    Kris: Anything else?

    Jason: I gave her some, but she still took mine.

    Kris: Daeisha, what do you think happened?

    Daeisha: He had all the playdough and just shared a little. So I took some so I could play too.

Jason: Daeisha had some. (Points to the little glob he gave her.)

Kris: Let's let Daeisha finish.

Daeisha: I needed more to play, so I took it.

Kris: Let's see, is this right? Jason, you were making a big nest with the playdough. Daeisha came and didn't have any. Jason gave Daeisha some. Daeisha, you didn't have enough, so you took more so you could play too?

Both children nod, which assures Kris that they both feel like they have been heard and are ready to move forward.

4. **Solves** the problem with the children—not for them.

Kris: So how can we fix this so you can both play?

Daeisha: He can share more.

Jason: But not too much.

Kris sets the playdough in front of Jason. Jason gives Daeisha a bit more. Daeisha and Kris both look at Jason. He grimaces but hands over enough to satisfy the other two.

Kris: Thank you, Jason. Can you still make a dinosaur nest or maybe just an eagle nest?

Jason: A littler dinosaur nest.

Kris: Daeisha, Jason was on the floor, and he was upset. He has given you more playdough. Seems like you need to do something here to make things better. (*Instead of forcing Daeisha to apologize, Kris guides the child to think about what would make Jason feel better.*)

Daeisha: Thank you, Jason. Sorry. Can I make you some eggs?

Jason: Yeah, a whole bunch.

5. **Follows up** with one or both children by having a *guidance talk.* Sitting next to Daeisha, Kris thanks her for helping to solve the problem and talks with her about what to do next time so no one is hurt. They agree that if a classmate won't share, Daeisha will ask a teacher for help.

Although guidance may seem time consuming, a scene like this can play out in just five minutes. If you truly do not have time to engage in all five steps at that moment, do steps one and two right away and tell the children when you will get together to finish the mediation. Don't forget! If the problem is no longer a big deal to both children when you get together, skip to step five for a guidance talk. Help each child learn how to get along better next time.

Seeing the Value of Guidance

Why is guidance well worth the time it takes? Here are four reasons.

First, the teacher does not make one child seem like a perpetrator and the other seem like a victim. Adults can actually start bully-victim patterns if they consistently comfort the "helpless" victim and punish the "guilty" perpetrator. Kris handled this situation so both children felt they were worthy individuals who belonged in the class and were capable of solving their problems and of learning from their mistakes.

Second, Kris worked *with* Daeisha. Children who have the boldness to take things from others most often also have the individual strength to become leaders who can work cooperatively with others (like Jeremiah), if we support them in developing their emotional and social skills. This change requires belief in the child and firm, friendly, and consistent guidance (with an emphasis on the friendly).

Third, every use of guidance provides powerful lessons in language arts and social studies. Children who learn to put strong emotions into non-hurtful words gain vocabulary and communication skills that serve them well for their entire lives. Children who learn the social studies lessons of overcoming differences and solving problems together are gaining democratic life skills.

Finally, every time members of an encouraging classroom see guidance at work, children and adults together learn the vital lesson that everyone is a worthy individual, belongs in the group, and can participate in solving problems. For all of us, this is important learning for making our democracy "more perfect."

Closing Thoughts

Guidance should not be thought of as a weak alternative to traditional discipline—it's being a good coach who doesn't give up on any member of the team. Your efforts at guidance don't have to be perfect, but if you persist and reflect, you will get good results. Like Beth and Kris, we learn even as we teach. Do these things, and you will feel positively about yourself as a teacher—and that will help with the inner calm you need to guide children toward healthy emotional and social skills.

Reflection Questions

1. When children have conflicts, what does it mean for them that guidance calms and teaches rather than punishes?

2. How does using guidance fit within your program's preschool curriculum?

3. How does moving from conventional discipline to early childhood guidance impact teachers' emotional responses to children?

4. A guidance approach may include preparing children by teaching and supporting clear rules and expectations with visual supports. How else might a guidance approach support the whole child?

About the Author

Dan Gartrell, EdD, is an emeritus professor of early childhood education and a former Head Start teacher. Dan wrote *Young Children*'s long-running "Guidance Matters" column between 2005 and 2014. He is also the author of seven books on guidance, including the second edition of *Education for a Civil Society: Teaching Young Children to Gain Five Democratic Life Skills* (NAEYC, 2023). To learn more, visit www.dangartrell.net.

The ideas explored in this article come from *Guidance with Every Child: Teaching Young Children to Manage Conflict* (Redleaf Press, 2017) and *A Guidance Guide for Early Childhood Leaders: Strengthening Relationships with Children, Families, and Colleagues* (Redleaf Press, 2020).

Photographs: pp. 74, 76, 77, 78 © Getty Images

Responses to Challenging Behavior

Why Some Common Strategies Don't Work and What to Do Instead

Keri Giordano, Emily Kokkinakis, and Briana Calcagno-Davi

Children's challenging behavior occurs for a variety of reasons. They may be frustrated by something they can't do yet (explain their feelings, write the first letter in their name), or they may be tired, hungry, sad, or just excited.

All behavior is trying to tell us something, so think about what might be causing or be connected to a child's behavior when deciding the best way to address it.

When faced with challenging behavior, **it's important to focus on teaching new skills and reinforcing desired behaviors.** When challenging behavior is replaced with appropriate skills, positive change is sure to follow!

Talented teachers who struggle with children's challenging behavior often turn to techniques they have observed, experienced, or been taught to use, only to discover that these methods don't work! Read on for practical, effective alternatives to try instead.

Use Logical Consequences

Instead of threatening to use a consequence that you can't or won't enforce ("If you do not clean up the blocks, I will remove them from the classroom") . . .

Try This

> Say what you mean and mean what you say. Be clear and consistent.

> Develop logical consequences, promise them, and use them. ("If you don't clean up the blocks, you can't use them anymore today.")

> Reinforce desired behaviors. ("Now no one will step on the blocks and get hurt.")

Why?

> Setting limits encourages children to test boundaries; it's how they learn what is and is not appropriate.

> When behavior is not followed by the promised consequence, limits become unclear and inconsistent. Children learn that you do not mean what you say (and will continue to test you).

Speak Calmly

Instead of speaking in a loud or threatening tone of voice . . .

Try This

> Take a minute so everyone can calm down.

> Speak quietly; bend down to the child's level.

> Calmly state the problem using "I messages." ("When children fight over toys, I feel afraid someone will get hurt.")

Why?

> Yelling isn't an effective way to communicate. Children hear your volume rather than your message.

> Yelling scares children and makes them feel unsupported. It affects a child's willingness to problem solve with you.

> Yelling may actually lead to an increase in undesired behaviors.

Allow Active Play Regardless of Behavior

Instead of keeping a child from participating in outside (or other active) time as a consequence of undesirable behavior . . .

Try This

> Review often with the children rules and expectations for recess. They should make sense to children and, ideally, be rules they have helped create.

> Acknowledge and reinforce desired behaviors.

> Apply logical consequences for breaking classroom and recess rules, such as limiting access to certain activities instead of denying a child recess altogether. For example, a child who jumps from the slide is not allowed to use the slide for the rest of the day.

Why?

> Missing recess deprives the brain of a necessary break (needed to reset and start fresh).

> Engaging in physical and unstructured play enhances children's cognitive, physical, and social and emotional development.

> Being physically active is a healthy outlet for energy that otherwise might contribute to challenging classroom behavior.

Discuss Issues Privately

Instead of posting charts in the classroom ranking each child's behavior (stoplight chart) . . .

Try This

> Discuss issues privately with children; be calm and supportive as you help them develop self-control.

> Have a planned set of logical consequences that you use consistently. ("If you crash Georgie's blocks, you need to move to a different center.")

> Rank the class as a whole, and use your observations as a reflection tool for the children. ("It sounds loud in here to me. What can we do to move the volume back to green?")

Why?

> Individual charts are embarrassing. Imagine your supervisor observing you teaching a lesson, then hanging a stoplight outside your door so everyone (children, parents, and other teachers) knows how well you did.

> Charts address undesired, rather than desired, behaviors. They don't speak to the underlying issue or teach a social skill.

Reinforce Appropriate Behavior

Instead of humiliating a child or hurting a child's feelings in an attempt to change a challenging behavior (saying "Do you need to go back to the baby class?" or writing names of children who do not listen on a board for the whole class to see) . . .

Try This

> Reinforce appropriate behaviors (sitting quietly during circle time) rather than shaming children for behaviors like being noisy and poking other children. Teach children the skills they're lacking, and give them opportunities to practice. Help a child recognize when they are feeling like they want to poke a friend and give them ideas of what to do instead—take a few breaths, roll their shoulders.

> If appropriate, ignore undesired behaviors.

Why?

> Children feel belittled and disrespected.

> Children may think teachers don't like them or resent the teachers who make them feel ashamed.

> Shaming gives children reasons to pick on peers.

Redirect

Instead of sending children to sit alone in an assigned space for a set period of time (time-out) to think about their behavior . . .

Try This

> Redirect the child toward a more appropriate behavior (walking instead of running). Be supportive—this is not a punishment!

> Teach effective and appropriate replacement skills. ("We ask when we want to use a friend's crayon.")

> Time-out is useful if it is child initiated; it should last only as long as it takes the child to calm down. Adults can give themselves time-outs (taking deep breaths and spending a few minutes away from children), and support children in learning to take a break.

Why?

> Time-out does not teach appropriate behavior skills. Children often engage in challenging behavior when they don't know more appropriate and effective ways to express themselves.

> Children might enjoy time-out and use it to escape from other activities.

Reflection Questions

1. What strategies have you tried in your classroom to address young children's challenging behavior that were unsuccessful? Looking back, what do you think could have made the strategy more successful?

2. What strategies have you tried that were successful? Why do you think they were successful? How can you apply this information to current behavior challenges you are facing?

3. Reflect on a time when you were supporting a child with challenging behavior. How did your emotions contribute to your responses or the responses of others?

Conclusion

Partner with families to let children know you are all working together to help them succeed. Tell parents about the behaviors you're seeing in the classroom and what strategies you're using so they can try those strategies at home. Ask parents what behaviors they see at home and collaborate to be consistent. Remember to stay positive.

Overall, to be successful, children need compassionate and caring adults who guide and support them. This leads to children learning appropriate, effective ways of expressing their feelings to get what they want and need.

About the Authors

Keri Giordano is an associate professor at Kean University. She has been in the field of early childhood since 1995 and specializes in working with children with challenging behavior and their teachers and families.

Emily Kokkinakis has worked with children and conducted research in early childhood settings. She currently works as a crisis specialist in Colorado and supports families after inpatient hospital admission.

Briana Calcagno-Davi is a pediatric neuropsychologist at Northwell Health. She has worked with children and families for over 15 years and specializes in medical and neurodevelopmental disorders.

Intensive and Individualized Practices

Even when preventive and targeted practices are implemented consistently, there may still be children who benefit from intensive and individualized supports to address persistent challenging behavior. These children may demonstrate behaviors that place them at risk for a social and emotional delay and may require special education services. At this level, a team-based approach is used to develop an individualized positive behavior support plan that incorporates a functional behavioral assessment (FBA). The goal of the FBA is to systematically gather data on the behaviors of concern to describe the *what*, *when*, *why,* and *how* (Fox, Strain, & Dunlap 2021). From this data, a comprehensive behavior intervention plan is developed in alignment with children's developmental goals (DEC 2017).

The three articles in this part discuss how to use a team-based approach as you develop and implement individualized behavior supports.

In "Becoming a Better Behavior Detective: Applying a Developmental and Contextual Lens on Behavior to Promote Social and Emotional Development," **Claire D. Vallotton, Jennifer A. Mortensen, Melissa M. Burnham, Kalli B. Decker,** and **Marjorie Beeghly** describe the need to incorporate the child's perspective when interpreting and responding to a behavior. The five-step reflective cycle explored in this article supports developing this critical and broader understanding of children's behavior.

Barbara Kaiser and **Judy Sklar Raminsky** provide a detailed account of the FBA process in their article, "Functional Assessment and Positive Behavior Support: The Role of Early Learning Program Leaders and Teachers." They explain how it works, how data collection occurs, and the roles and responsibilities of specific team members.

In the final article, **Anne M. Butler** and **Michaelene M. Ostrosky** pay particular attention to the role of a child's family on the team. "Reducing Challenging Behavior During Transitions: Strategies for Early Childhood Educators to Share with Parents" highlights approaches and strategies that work in early learning programs and can also support families whose young children have difficulty with transitions across routines and activities in the home setting.

REFERENCES

DEC (Division for Early Childhood). 2017. "Challenging Behavior and Young Children." Position statement. Washington, DC: DEC. www.decdocs.org/position-statement-challenging-beha.

Fox, L., P.S. Strain, & G. Dunlap. 2021. "Preventing the Use of Preschool Suspension and Expulsion: Implementing the Pyramid Model." *Preventing School Failure: Alternative Education for Children and Youth* 65 (4): 312–22.

Becoming a Better Behavior Detective

Applying a Developmental and Contextual Lens on Behavior to Promote Social and Emotional Development

Claire D. Vallotton, Jennifer A. Mortensen, Melissa M. Burnham, Kalli B. Decker, and Marjorie Beeghly

Ms. Carrie notices 24-month-old Riley run over to Casey, an 18-month-old who is playing quietly in the soft toys area, covering the baby dolls with blankets. Riley reaches for one of the dolls, and Casey scratches Riley's arm, drawing blood. Riley shoves Casey, grabs the doll, then runs away, taking the doll to another part of the classroom. Casey watches Riley run away with the doll, then starts to cry loudly. This is the third time today that Riley has taken a toy from another child, and the second time today that Casey has drawn blood. Ms. Carrie must decide how to appropriately respond to their behaviors.

This scene is familiar to any early childhood educator who has spent time with infants and toddlers in group settings. The abilities to regulate emotions and behavior develop slowly over time, beginning in infancy. Infants and toddlers experience a growing range of intense emotions, but they cannot understand and regulate these feelings on their own; they need trusted adults to help organize their feelings by responding to their needs quickly, appropriately, and compassionately (Beeghly & Tronick 2011). This support guides very young children on how to calm their bodies and to express their emotions in healthy ways using newfound behaviors (such as resting in a cozy spot) and using emerging verbal and cognitive abilities (such as recognizing and naming feelings).

No matter how well we use preventive strategies to avoid altercations such as the one between Riley and Casey, they are bound to occur. How we interpret and how we respond to young children's behavior are part of the daily work of infant and toddler teachers. In a situation such as the opening vignette, early childhood educators can draw on knowledge of child development and reflection skills to detect what is underlying the child's behavior and to determine a response. Sharpening our "behavior detective" skills requires us to use reflective practices to apply our knowledge of development in service of understanding the individual infant or toddler.

This article presents ways to systematically apply a developmental and contextual lens to understand young children's behavior. We describe a five-step reflective cycle (see page 88) for implementing and reflecting on relationship-based guidance strategies to foster infants' and toddlers' social and emotional development. We will outline each step and describe how early childhood educators can enact them.

Step One: What Is the Child Doing? What Are They Feeling?

For early education professionals, scaffolding emotion regulation is as critical as any academic skill. To best support development, reflective practices such as "observe, listen, wonder, and respond" (Weatherston 2013, 62) enhance a teacher's ability to see and feel the world from the child's perspective. Our relationships with children form the basis for how we respond to their behaviors; at the same time, our knowledge of children's families, temperament, and other characteristics may interfere with our ability to see the child clearly. Thus, our reflective cycle starts by carefully observing a child's behaviors and facial expressions, by listening to their voices and words, and by systematically asking ourselves a set of questions to help us consider, and reconsider, the child's perspective:

> What is the child doing?

> What is the child feeling?

> What is the child trying to communicate?

> Is this behavior developmentally appropriate for the child's age (NAEYC 2020, 2022)?

> What is the child's body posture and facial expression?

> What is the child's tone of voice?

> Does the child need a caregiver?

5-Step Reflective Cycle

1 **What is the child doing? What are they feeling?**

Observe and describe the child's behavior, facial expressions, vocal/verbal cues. Wonder about the child's feelings, desires, thoughts, and intentions.

2 **What is the child responding to?**

Take the child's perspective: what are the developmental and contextual factors the child might be responding to, including internal and external factors?

3 **What is the child's underlying need?**

Identify the child's underlying feelings and need(s), given their development, context, and feelings.

4 **How can I respond to meet the child's underlying needs?**

Respond in a way that meets the child's underlying emotional and relational needs in this context.

5 **Was my response what the child needed?**

Reflect on the child's reaction to your response. Did your response meet the child's need? How else could you have responded?

While some situations may demand a response right away, many situations would benefit from pausing to consider the underlying reasons for behavior before responding. Even if you must respond right away, taking time to think about the children's behavior shortly afterward may give you new insights and will help you respond in the most supportive way in the future.

Step Two: What Is the Child Responding To?

Having observed and pondered what a child is doing and feeling, an educator using a developmental and contextual lens next considers the internal and external factors that may be influencing an infant's or toddler's behavior. It is crucial to think about a young child's experiences both in and outside the early learning setting and to ensure that we seek insights about each child through trusting, reciprocal relationships with their family.

When a concerning behavior arises, there are seven possible factors that—on their own or in combination—may be influencing the child at a particular time (see "Behavior Influences and Self-Reflection Questions" on page 90). Following an ecological systems perspective (Bronfenbrenner 1992), we start by examining what is most proximal to the child, in time and space, then move out from there, applying our behavior detective lens to all of these factors, including

> The child's immediate or proximal experiences (physical well-being, immediate contexts, and day-to-day experiences)

> Who the child is (their developmental stage and temperament)

> The child's relationships to others (secure relationships, home and community cultures)

> The role that adverse experiences may be playing in the child's behavior

Physical First!

We must consider physical states and needs first because they are the baseline for child behavior. Infants and toddlers often do not have the words to express their feelings and needs, so our detective work begins there. Are they hungry or tired? Could they be teething or sick? Only after ruling out these types of possibilities do we consider the next six influences.

Context

The safety, stimulation, and security of the child's immediate context affect behavior, whether at home or in an early childhood setting (Rijlaardsam et al. 2013). Safety is created when environments and routines are predictable, reasonably calm, and children can explore without danger. In an unsafe or unsecure environment, children may have difficulty concentrating and may easily become overstimulated and distressed. Environments should offer playful, engaging learning opportunities with regular breaks. When children are not appropriately engaged, they seek out their own opportunities, which can lead to challenging and inappropriate behavior.

Therefore, a key question in this step asks whether a child is sufficiently engaged and appropriately stimulated by the environment. What is going on in the child's immediate context right now? Are there enough interesting materials and activities available? Are the teachers actively engaging with the children?

Developmental Progressions and Waves

Development proceeds in a series of bursts and regressions, like waves, rather than as a smooth line (Brazelton Touchpoints Center 2008; NAEYC 2020), which can mean our expectations of children may become misaligned if we do not take into account when they are experiencing a shift. We must always ask whether our expectations of children's behavior are aligned with the current developmental skills we have seen from them across all domains. Frustrations arise when children's desires outpace their current capabilities. Toddlers often understand more than they can say and may become distressed when they cannot express their wants to others. In addition, regressions, which are temporary periods when a child's nervous system is reorganizing as they gain new skills, often come with increased fussiness and disruptions in sleep, feeding, and self-regulation (Scher & Cohen 2015). For children with delays or disabilities, these uneven profiles may be more pronounced and developmental transitions prolonged, leading to more extended periods of disorganization. Framed by a developmental and contextual lens, teachers can more accurately identify, interpret, and support infants and toddlers as they experience significant developmental shifts (Singer 2007; Sparrow 2018).

Behavior Influences and Self-Reflection Questions

Step 2: What is the child responding to?	
Influence	**Sample questions to ask yourself and families**
1 **Physical first!**	Is the child hungry, tired, cold/hot, uncomfortable, or in pain? Were the child's care routines disrupted today or yesterday? Is the child teething, sick, or constipated? Are the child's senses overwhelmed by the social or physical environment?
2 **Context**	What is going on in the classroom/immediate context right now? Is the current environment overstimulating—too noisy, too bright, too unpredictable? Are there too many people in the room? Has there been a change in the physical or social environment, or daily routines in the classroom? What is going on at home right now? Has the family moved or made another big change?
3 **Developmental progressions and waves**	What developmental shifts is the child making that could influence this behavior? Are they in a new phase of attachment to educators? Is the child just learning to sit, crawl, or walk independently? Are they starting to develop and assert their autonomy or independence?
4 **Temperament**	How adaptable is this child to changes in general? Is this child highly reactive or easily overwhelmed, showing quick and strong reactions to changes in activities or in the environment?
5 **Secure relationships**	Does the child have at least one caregiver in the classroom who is a safe haven and secure base? Is that trusted person present and available? Has there been a disruption in the child's family relationships (through divorce or separation, death, arrival of a new sibling, or a new parent)?
6 **Culture**	How does the child's family culture value and socialize this behavior? Is there consistency between how educators respond to this behavior at home and in school? Could a mismatch between home and school in practices or communication behaviors affect this behavior?
7 **Stress and trauma**	Has there been a recent increase in stress or chaos in the child's life? Did the child experience or witness violence, disaster, or physical harm? Is the child able to seek comfort and safety from educators?

Adapted, with permission, from C.D. Vallotton, H. Brophy-Herb, L. Roggman, R. Chazan-Cohen, & CUPID (Collaborative for Understanding the Pedagogy of Infant/Toddler Development, *Working Well with Babies: Comprehensive Competencies for Educators of Infants and Toddlers* (St. Paul, MN: Redleaf, 2021).

Temperament

All children differ in temperament, the biological set point that influences behavioral style. Displays of temperaments range from easy-going, adaptable, and predictable to reactive, fussy, and irregular. A young child with a less-adaptive temperament stands to gain the most developmentally when caregivers truly understand their behavior and how it affects a child's experiences, and the adults respond in supportive ways (Pluess & Belsky 2010).

Secure Relationships

Attachment is the special bond that develops between young children and important caregivers and is foundational for learning and behavior. A child with secure attachments uses their caregivers as a secure base for exploration and as a safe haven in times of distress. Both are key in helping infants organize and regulate their feelings.

Infants and toddlers are affected by the absence or loss of a familiar early childhood educator in a group setting, and family changes can disrupt a child's sense of security. When presented with challenging behavior, we should consider whether any changes or disruptions have occurred in attachment relationships at home or in the early childhood setting.

Culture

Infant and toddler behavior is influenced by the cultural beliefs and values of both their families and early childhood professionals. These influences can manifest in subtle ways, such as in how physical and social environments are shaped, in beliefs about childrearing including sleeping and feeding practices (Rogoff, Dahl, & Callanan 2018), and in communication styles. For example, in some cultures, it is not respectful for a child to make eye contact with an adult; in other cultures, it is disrespectful for adults to put a hand on the top of a child's head.

When presented with behavior that elicits surprise, concern, or disapproval on the part of the educator, consider whether this behavior might reflect a child's cultural contexts at home and in the community. This is not something a teacher can decipher alone; the best way to learn about each child's culture is through strong and ongoing connections with their family and community. This includes asking about the family's hopes and priorities for their child and about what they would like to share about their culture or home life (Rogoff, Dahl, & Callanan 2018). Also, an early childhood educator must recognize and continually reflect on how their own culture and identity influence their thinking and practices (NAEYC 2019).

Stress and Trauma

Our understanding of stress and trauma, and their effects on brain development, social and emotional development, and behavior, is growing rapidly. Predictable and moderate amounts of stress (e.g., mild family conflict, a sibling's birth) are a typical part of growing up and can help build resilience (Beeghly & Tronick 2011; Perry 2007). Unpredictable, unrelenting stress (e.g., neglect, physical harm, long-term caregiver separation), also known as toxic stress, with little caregiver support can adversely affect brain development and prompt intense reactions and behaviors, such as unpredictable expressions of anger and frustration or regressions that do not self-correct in a short period of time (National Scientific Council on the Developing Child 2005/2014; Perry 2007). For these children especially, teachers must be consistent, predictable, and maintain safe, affectionate relationships (Perry 2014). Indeed, a child's ability to manage stress is dependent on the quality of relationships with caregivers (Lally & Mangione 2017). (For more information about working with children experiencing trauma, see also Norman et al. 2021.)

Most infants and toddlers do not experience toxic stress. Thus, most challenging behavior in the classroom will be better understood in light of the other listed influences, which is why stress and trauma are listed last here. Although toxic stress and trauma can influence a child's social and emotional development, there can be a tendency to attribute any intense emotion or dysregulated behavior (such as intense aggression) exclusively to these adverse experiences. Above all, early childhood educators should take care to avoid blaming or labeling children and instead take a comprehensive view of the social and emotional expressions that children demonstrate.

Step Three: What Is the Child's Emotion and Underlying Need?

Most negative expressions of emotion are typical for a very young child who is just figuring out the world with limited language, with uncontrollable feelings, and while navigating shared spaces with peers (Gross 2015). Step three involves integrating our observation of the child's behavior and emotions (step one) and our interpretation of what the child is responding to (step two)—rooted in knowledge of the child and family—to determine what the child needs in a particular situation.

At this step, it is helpful to remind ourselves how we might act if we were feeling this way and did not have adult perspective or coping skills; sometimes *we* act out, even *with* adult coping skills and perspective! "Linking Emotions, Expressions, and Needs" (on page 93) connects children's emotional experiences with what they need from us, such as a need to feel safe or connected and loved.

Step Four: How Can I Respond to Meet the Child's Underlying Needs?

Early childhood educators are critical attachment figures for young children, and this relationship offers the young child safety and security, a place to express emotions and to learn about appropriate behaviors (Mortensen & Barnett 2015). Using developmentally appropriate strategies, teachers can promote infants' and toddlers' social and emotional development through three relationship-based strategies: touch, togetherness talk, and "time in." (See "Strategies to Build Relationships Through Guidance While Promoting Child Compliance" on page 94.) For example, in the opening vignette, after

Linking Emotions, Expressions, and Needs

Step 3: What is the child's emotion and underlying need?		
What the child feels	**What the child needs**	**What the teacher can do**
Frustration	I need to feel capable of accomplishing my goal.	Acknowledge my feelings. Help me find a solution to the problem so I can reach my goal.
Anger	I need to feel understood and validated.	Tell me it's okay to feel this way. Help me find safe ways to express my feelings. If possible, help me find a solution to the problem.
Overwhelmed	I need to feel held and contained.	Help me find spaces that calm me. Spend one-on-one time with me.
Sadness and grief	I need to feel connected and loved.	Comfort me. Invite me to interact. Help me find ways to soothe myself, but let me feel sad for as long as I need to.
Fear and anxiety	I need to feel safe.	Let me know you will protect me. Make my environment, routines, and adult behavior calm and predictable.

attending to Riley's wound and returning the doll to Casey, their teacher Ms. Carrie might sit down with Riley and read a favorite book together. Another teacher might sit close to Casey and gently stroke Casey's arm, talking about the use of gentle hands.

Step Five: Was My Response What the Child Needed?

As educators, we learn not only from our experiences in the moments of teaching but also from reflection. Reflecting on our interactions with children is a foundational part of professional development and continuous growth. In earlier steps, we described several reflective practices: observing behavior (step one), pausing to integrate knowledge before responding (steps two and three), and implementing our response thoughtfully (step four). Step five asks us to reflect on the effects of our responses on the child's well-being and in meeting their needs. This use of reflective practice, using a developmental and contextual lens, can strengthen the educator-child relationship overall.

Through reflection we gain insights into the ways we influence children's behavior, which can be used to plan ahead to prevent future challenges and to ensure that we intervene in consistent and responsive ways over time. To do so, we can ask ourselves: Was the child's need met? How did the child's behavior influence me? How have I responded in the past? What did I learn about the child and myself in this interaction? How can I connect with the child's family to gain their insights about how their child's needs may have been met differently during the interaction?

Strategies to Build Relationships Through Guidance While Promoting Child Compliance

Step 4: How can I respond to meet the child's underlying needs?		
Do this	**Not this**	**Because . . .**
Touch: Move close to the child and use gentle, respectful, affectionate touch to get the child's attention and connect.	› Talk/yell across a room › Sudden or rough touch	Gentle, affectionate touch is calming, it reinforces the child's trust in your relationship, and it helps the child feel connected, which promotes willingness to comply. Some children may react negatively to touch when they are very upset; teachers should use knowledge of individual children in making this choice.
Togetherness talk: Refer to the child's connection to you or the classroom/community, such as "Let's clean up together." "We use gentle touches with our classmates."	› Talk about the child's behavior to others › Direct the child to do things on their own	Togetherness talk expresses guidance as a common goal. Children are more likely to go along with what we ask when they are working with us on a goal, rather than forced to comply with an adult's goal.
Time in: When children experience and act on strong emotions, spend time with them one-on-one if possible, making yourself physically and emotionally available. If you must stay with other children, move close to the child who is upset, while giving them some space if they need it.	› Time out in any form, such as sitting in a corner, going to another room, being sent away from a desired activity	"Time in" provides children time with a trusted caregiver for connection and comfort. It supports the child to move from a highly aroused negative emotional state (angry tantrum) to a calm, connected state so that they can change their behavior. Time out isolates children, which is less effective in helping to calm them, and can produce feelings of shame.

Clearing Our View

We all come to our work with infants and toddlers with different experiences, values, and beliefs, including biases, that may cloud our lenses, making the process of becoming a behavior detective more challenging. Sometimes biases are visible to us, but most often they lurk outside of our awareness or direct attention. For example, thinking back to the opening scene, what did you think about the gender of Riley and Casey or their other social identities related to race, ethnicity, economic class, or different abilities?

We all make certain automatic assumptions about children and their behavior. Recent evidence suggests that when teachers find explanations for behavior that are outside the child's classroom experiences—particularly when they do not feel qualified or prepared to respond to challenging behavior or needs—they are more likely to recommend expulsion and other exclusionary practices (Martin, Bosk, & Bailey 2018). A child's race and gender, among other social identities, can directly play into these decisions: for example, preservice and in-service early care practitioners are more likely to look at the behavior of children of color (Gilliam et al. 2016) and attribute their behavior as problematic (Okonofua & Eberhardt 2015). In our experiences training preservice early childhood educators, when posed with vignettes about children's behavior, they also are more likely to attribute negative behaviors to factors involving a child's home and traumatic experiences when featuring a child of color.

Thus, even when we are thoughtful about the potential reasons underlying children's behavior, we are all vulnerable to applying our developmental and contextual lenses unevenly and inaccurately across children and families. Early childhood educators should reflect on their relationships with each family and put concerted effort into building relationships that help them to more clearly connect with and understand each child's family. Clearing our lenses helps us to be present and effective for all children.

Moving Ahead: Using a Detective Lens to Plan, Prevent, and Respond

Riley is huddled in the book area of the classroom, softly crying while holding the captured doll. Her arm has stopped bleeding. Ms. Carrie gently touches her shoulder and says, "Oh, you have a scratch on your arm! I'm sorry that happened. Let's go clean it up and get a bandage." Riley drops the doll and turns to Ms. Carrie with outreached arms.

After tending to the wound, they walk hand-in-hand back to the book area and pick up the doll. "Let's go deliver this back to Casey," Ms. Carrie says. "She was playing with this one." Riley reluctantly follows to where Casey is seated, now covering the toy cars with blankets. Ms. Carrie offers the doll to Casey, and she adds it to the line of cars waiting to be covered. Ms. Carrie finds a similar doll and hands it to Riley. "Here's one for you!" With the two girls watching Ms. Carrie, she points to Riley's bandage, gently strokes her arm, and says, "Look, Casey, Riley needed a bandage for her arm. We need to be gentle with our classmates. Now that you both have dolls, do you want to play together?" Ms. Carrie offers Riley a blanket from a nearby bin in case she'd like to engage in the play Casey has begun. The two children smile as they cover their dolls.

Ms. Carrie makes a note to change the dramatic play area so that all the dolls are displayed rather than stored in a closed bin. She also wants to ask Casey's parent if anything is happening at home that might be influencing Casey's reactive scratching.

Reflecting and Planning Ahead

No matter how confident the teacher was in her response to Riley and Casey, it is always worthwhile to revisit the interaction. Looking back, we see that Ms. Carrie observed Riley's behavior and the emotions (huddling, crying) and what she was responding to (the scratch on her arm from Casey), but she did not label these out loud for Riley in order to help build Riley's understanding of her own feelings. Ms. Carrie identified Riley's underlying need to be comforted physically and emotionally, and responded warmly with touch (holding hands), togetherness talk ("Let's go . . ."), and time together (caring for Riley's wound, taking the doll to Casey and talking afterward).

Questions to Guide Personal Reflection

Moving forward: Using your reflections to prevent behaviors and plan ahead	
Context	**Questions**
Examine a recent event in the classroom together	› What could have been a different interpretation of the child's behaviors, responses, or needs? › What might have influenced my interpretation or response? Could my interpretation of the child's behavior be related to the child's characteristics such as gender, race, ethnicity, economic class, or culture? › What information about this event should I share with the child's family? Is there more information I may want to gather from them that may help me understand the child's behaviors, responses, strengths, or needs? › What other types of responses could I have considered using with this child?
Examine the supports that are available or that may be needed	› How am I using the support I currently have (specialists, coteachers, supervisors, administrators)? › Is there someone else I can lean into to share the responsibility or for guidance and support? › What types of supports would help me have the kinds of interactions I want with children (collegial, supervisory, professional development experiences and materials)? › Am I getting the support I need?
Examine ways in which you may need to advocate for yourself	› What actions can I take to advocate for myself? › How can I take care of myself right now?

But what was Casey experiencing that caused her to scratch Riley? And what can be done to prevent this type of incident in the future? Ms. Carrie made a plan to change the dramatic play area to eliminate the competition over the dolls and to ask Casey's family about any similar behavior they might have noticed at home. What information might be shared with each child's family, and what questions may help Ms. Carrie better understand each child? While Ms. Carrie could ask herself these questions in a time of self-reflection, talking them over with others could provide additional insights. Reflecting with coworkers and supervisors is a final component of becoming a better behavior detective, turning the lens on ourselves so that we understand not just the children's behavior, but our own as well.

Conclusion

As early education practitioners, we prioritize the needs of children. Yet, we must also reflect on our own experiences and needs to support both personal well-being and professional development. This type of reflection allows us to become more self-aware, which makes us more comfortable exploring what guides our responses to children, asking for support from others, and advocating for our own needs.

Educators who regularly engage in reflective practices may learn to recognize how their own emotional reactions influence interactions with children; this self-reflection in relation to children helps us bring our real selves to the classroom and be truly emotionally present. (To learn more, see Hatton-Bowers et al. 2021.) Knowledge of both self and others develops over time as a result of regular reflective practice.

Reflective practices are intended to be cyclical with early childhood educators observing, reflecting, responding, then cycling back to observing (Vallotton et al. 2021). Reflective practices are more effective and easier to maintain over time when supported by other professionals, including supervisors or coaches (Bernstein & Edwards 2012), coteachers, or a professional learning community. Given the high level of stress faced by early education practitioners (Smith & Lawrence 2019), reflective practices can play an important part in supporting educators' own mental health (Jennings et al. 2013) and abilities to respond to children in developmentally supportive ways (Amini Virmani & Ontai 2010; Brophy-Herb et al. 2019; Jennings et al. 2017; Weigand 2007). "Questions to Guide Personal Reflection" on page 96 can be used on your own, or with colleagues or a supervisor, to turn your behavior detective lens on yourself and to support your continued growth as an early childhood education professional.

Reflection Questions

1. When you are working to better understand children's behavior, when and how do you examine your own perspective about the behavior? How do you reflect on challenging behavior from the child's perspective?

2. How do you share information and collaborate with families to help children communicate more effectively with others?

3. How might you assess what you are communicating to the child and whether or not it meets the child's needs?

REFERENCES

Amini Virmani, E., & L. Ontai. 2010. "Supervision and Training in Child Care: Does Reflective Supervision Foster Caregiver Insightfulness?" *Infant Mental Health Journal* 31 (1): 16–32.

Beeghly, M., & E. Tronick. 2011. "Early Resilience in the Context of Parent–Infant Relationships: A Social Developmental Perspective." *Current Problems in Pediatric and Adolescent Health Care* 41 (7): 197–201.

Bernstein, V., & R. Edwards. 2012. "Supporting Early Childhood Practitioners Through Relationship-Based, Reflective Supervision." *NHSA Dialog* 15 (3): 286–301.

Brazelton Touchpoints Center. 2008. "A Review of Early Care and Education Literature: Evidence Base for Touchpoints." Executive summary. Boston: Brazelton Touchpoints Center. www.brazeltontouchpoints.org/wp-content/uploads/2011/09/A_Review_of_the_Early_Care_and_Education_Literature__Evidence_Base_Oct_20081.pdf.

Brophy-Herb, H., A. Williamson, G. Cook, J. Torquati, K. Decker, J. Vu, C. Vallotton, & L. Duncan. 2019. "Preservice Students' Dispositional Mindfulness and Developmentally Supportive Practices with Infants and Toddlers." *Mindfulness* 10 (4): 759–68.

Bronfenbrenner, U. 1992. "Ecological Systems Theory." In *Six Theories of Child Development: Revised Formulations and Current Issues*, ed. R. Vasta, 187–249. Philadelphia: Jessica Kingsley.

Gilliam, W.S., A.N. Maupin, C.R. Reyes, M. Accavitti, & F. Shic. 2016. "Do Early Educators' Implicit Biases Regarding Sex and Race Relate to Behavior Expectations and Recommendations of Preschool Expulsions and Suspensions?" *Yale University Child Study Center* 9 (28): 1–16.

Gross, J.J. 2015. "Emotion Regulation: Current Status and Future Prospects." *Psychological Inquiry* 26 (1): 1–26.

Hatton-Bowers, H., E.A. Virmani, L. Nathans, B.A. Walsh, M.J. Buell, P. Lanzon, S.I. Plata-Potter, & L.A. Roe. 2021. "Bringing Your Real Self to the Classroom." *Young Children* 76 (1): 30–34.

Jennings, P., J. Frank, K. Snowberg, M. Coccia, & M. Greenberg. 2013. "Improving Classroom Learning Environments by Cultivating Awareness and Resilience in Education (CARE): Results of a Randomized Controlled Trial." *School Psychology Quarterly* 28 (4): 374–90.

Jennings, P., J. Brown, J. Frank, S. Doyle, Y. Oh, R. Davis, D. Rasheed, A. DeWeese, A. DeMauro, H. Cham, & M. Greenberg. 2017. "Improving Classroom Learning Environments by Cultivating Awareness and Resilience in Education (CARE): Results of a Randomized Controlled Trial." *Journal of Educational Psychology* 109 (7): 1010–28.

Lally, J., & P. Mangione. 2017. "Caring Relationships: The Heart of Early Brain Development." *Young Children* 72 (2): 17–24.

Martin, K., E. Bosk, & D. Bailey. 2018. "Teachers' Perceptions of Childcare and Preschool Expulsion." *Children & Society* 32 (2): 87–97.

Mortensen, J.A., & M.A. Barnett. 2015. "Teacher–Child Interactions in Infant/Toddler Child Care and Socioemotional Development." *Early Education and Development* 26 (2): 209–29.

NAEYC. 2019. "Advancing Equity in Early Childhood Education." Position statement. Washington, DC: NAEYC. www.naeyc.org/resources/position-statements/equity.

NAEYC. 2020. "Developmentally Appropriate Practice (DAP)." Position statement. Washington, DC: NAEYC. www.naeyc.org/resources/position-statements/dap.

NAEYC. 2022. *Developmentally Appropriate Practice in Early Childhood Programs Serving Children from Birth Through Age 8.* 4th ed. Washington, DC: NAEYC.

National Scientific Council on the Developing Child. 2005/2014. "Excessive Stress Disrupts the Architecture of the Developing Brain." Working Paper 3. Updated ed. Cambridge, MA: Center on the Developing Child at Harvard University. https://developingchild.harvard.edu/wp-content/uploads/2005/05/Stress_Disrupts_Architecture_Developing_Brain-1.pdf.

Norman, V.J., A.C. Juhasz, K.N. Useche, & K.M. Kinniburgh. 2021. "How Are You Feeling? Strategies for Helping Children Understand and Manage Emotions." *Young Children* 76 (1): 63–68.

Okonofua, J.A., & J.L. Eberhardt. 2015. "Two Strikes: Race and the Disciplining of Young Students." *Psychological Science* 26 (5): 617–24.

Perry, B. 2007. "Stress, Trauma, and Post-Traumatic Stress in Young Children." *Child Trauma Academy.* https://7079168e-705a-4dc7-be05-2218087aa989.filesusr.com/ugd/aa51c7_60c617d2160b417d9ee0f80e5ca8eaac.pdf.

Perry, B. 2014. "Helping Traumatized Children: A Brief Overview for Caregivers." *Child Trauma Academy.* https://7079168e-705a-4dc7-be05-2218087aa989.filesusr.com/ugd/aa51c7_237459a7e16b4b7e9d2c4837c908eefe.pdf.

Pluess, M., & J. Belsky. 2010. "Differential Susceptibility to Parenting and Quality Child Care." *Developmental Psychology* 46 (2): 379–90.

Rijlaarsdam, J., H. Tiemeier, A. Hofman, V.W. Jaddoe, J.P. Mackenbach, F.C. Verhulst, & G.W. Stevens. 2013. "Home Environments of Infants: Relations with Child Development Through Age 3." *Journal of Epidemiology and Community Health* 67 (1): 14–20.

Rogoff, B., A. Dahl, & M. Callanan. 2018. "The Importance of Understanding Children's Lived Experiences." *Developmental Review* 50: 5–15.

Scher, A., & D. Cohen. 2015. "Sleep as a Mirror of Developmental Transitions in Infancy: The Case of Crawling." *Monographs of the Society for Research in Child Development* 80 (1): 70–88.

Singer, J. 2007. "The Brazelton Touchpoints Approach to Infants and Toddlers in Care: Foundation for a Lifetime of Learning and Loving." *Dimensions of Early Childhood* 35 (3): 4–11.

Smith, S., & S. Lawrence. 2019. *Early Care and Education Teacher Well-Being: Associations with Children's Experience, Outcomes, and Workplace Conditions: A Research-to-Policy Brief.* New York: Child Care & Early Education Research Connections.

Sparrow, J. 2018. "Berry Brazelton's Contributions to Research, Policy, and Practice." *Young Children* 73 (3): 6–9.

Vallotton, C.D., H. Brophy-Herb, L. Roggman, R. Chazan-Cohen, & CUPID (Collaborative for Understanding the Pedagogy of Infant/Toddler Development). 2021. *Working Well with Babies: Comprehensive Competencies for Educators of Infants and Toddlers.* St. Paul, MN: Redleaf.

Weatherston, D. 2013. "Reflective Practice: Look, Listen, Wonder, and Respond." *ZERO TO THREE* 33 (3): 62–65.

Weigand, R. 2007. "Reflective Supervision in Child Care." *ZERO TO THREE* 28 (2): 17–22.

About the Authors

Claire D. Vallotton, PhD, is professor of human development and family studies at Michigan State University. She is the founding coordinator of the Collaborative for Understanding the Pedagogy of Infant/Toddler Development (CUPID), and the lead author of a book representing CUPID's work, *Working Well with Babies: Comprehensive Competencies for Educators of Infants and Toddlers*.

Jennifer A. Mortensen, PhD, CFLE, is associate professor in the College of Education and Human Development at the University of Nevada, Reno. Her research focuses on the well-being of families with infants and toddlers, including the role of early care and home visiting settings in supporting both parents and children.

Melissa M. Burnham, PhD, is professor of human development and family science at the University of Nevada, Reno. Melissa has been engaged in research, teaching, and policy related to early care and education for the past 19 years.

Kalli B. Decker, PhD, is associate professor of human development and family science at Montana State University in Bozeman, Montana. Kalli's research primarily focuses on early intervention services for young children with additional support needs and their families.

Marjorie Beeghly, PhD, is professor of psychology at Wayne State University in Detroit, Michigan. Her research examines how biological and social characteristics alter the trajectories of communicative and social and emotional development in infants and young children at risk for developmental problems due to their exposure to stressors.

Functional Assessment and Positive Behavior Support

The Role of Early Learning Program Leaders and Teachers

Barbara Kaiser and Judy Sklar Rasminsky

Schools and centers across the country use positive behavior support (PBS) as a universal, whole-school approach to create a positive school climate and prevent challenging behavior (Samuels 2013). PBS is a tiered strategy, meaning that it recognizes that different children have different levels of need for support and intervention. In order to help the 1 to 7 percent of those who require a more intensive, individualized approach, PBS is often paired with a technique called functional assessment or functional analysis (FA) or functional behavioral assessment (FBA).

Developed by behavioral psychologists, FA enables educators to observe a child more closely and collect data that illuminates why the challenging behavior is occurring at a particular time in a particular place. With this information, it becomes possible to create an individual positive behavior support plan for the child.

The most important idea behind both strategies is that challenging behavior is a child's solution to a problem, and this behavior enables them to fulfill their needs. With the help of careful observation and the behavior incident reports staff members have collected, FA allows teachers to figure out the purpose or function of the behavior as well as the events that trigger and maintain it.

With this information, program staff can create a behavior support plan that will empower them to teach the child more acceptable ways to get what they need. Although an FA and behavior support plan are similar to an Individualized Education Program (IEP), their use is not limited to children with disabilities, but like an IEP they may require parental permission and are always most effective when families are engaged in the process.

If a program feels that an FA and behavior support plan would be useful for a particular child, its team members have a few options. They can conduct the FA themselves and build a behavior support plan together with the child's family. If a psychologist or social worker is already working with the child, they may be willing to become part of the team and observe and record the child's behavior as well. Or staff could call in an outside expert from the local school board or one of the many agencies that deal with children's mental health, the local resource and referral agency, or the department of early learning in the area.

How Does Functional Assessment Work?

FA postulates that there are three possible functions or purposes for a challenging behavior (O'Neill et al. 2015):

> To obtain an object or attention

> To avoid a person or task

> To change the level of stimulation (Karsh et al. 1995)

But discovering which of these possible functions applies in a particular child's situation is a complex affair involving data. It usually takes a team that includes a program leader, the family, and anyone else who works with the child, including teachers and teaching assistants, an after-school teacher, a psychologist, or a social worker, plus a lot of observation, interviews, and discussion (Fox & Duda 2015).

To determine the function or purpose of a child's challenging behavior, the team usually employs a method called an A-B-C analysis (Bijou, Peterson, & Ault 1968).

› *A* stands for *antecedents*, which occur just before the challenging behavior and act as a trigger for it—for example, a teacher's demands or requests, difficult tasks, or transitions (O'Neill et al. 2015).

› *B* stands for the child's specific challenging *behavior*, which must be described clearly enough for anyone on the team to recognize and measure its intensity and frequency without any subjective interpretation (O'Neill et al. 2015). It might be spitting, hitting the teacher, or running out of the room.

› *C* stands for *consequences*, which are the responses to the challenging behavior. They can be anything that follows it, including the reactions of the other children or the teacher, and because they usually reward the behavior, they are often called the *maintaining consequences*. Laughing, offering attention (either positive or negative), removing the child from an activity, even providing help can all be maintaining consequences.

It is important to keep in mind that completing an FA is key to identifying the rationale behind a child's behavior, so the more people who are trained and available to participate in this exercise, the clearer the picture will become.

Observing Children

Information in the child's file and the behavior incident reports are a good place to start. But detailed observation of the child and the environment are the most important factors in identifying the function or purpose of challenging behavior.

Finding the time and ways to observe a child's challenging behavior as well as its antecedents and consequences are daunting tasks even for teachers with degrees, who may or may not have learned to observe and record behavior properly. And because teaching young children is in itself so task intensive, teachers may be concerned that they are already stretched to the limit. Nonetheless, they are probably the best possible observers because when an outside consultant enters the room, that person will certainly alter the behavior of the child or the educator or both. (Of course, after a couple of visits, they will not be as obtrusive, and their knowledge of the whole process of FA and positive behavior support will help the team to work more smoothly and effectively.) Program leaders can do observations too, and if they have been in the classroom regularly and often enough, their presence should not affect anyone else's behavior.

What Do Teams Need to Look For?

Before observing and recording the challenging behavior, the first step is to identify the exact **behaviors** that everyone is observing. Teachers often use general terms such as "defiant" or "aggressive," but this language is not specific enough. It is much clearer to say that the child hits, kicks, screams, withdraws, or refuses to follow directions.

This precision will help the team to determine the **antecedents** of the behavior. Was the child busy playing when the teacher said it was time to clean up? Were the other children too close to the child? Had the teacher been paying attention to their peers but not to them? Was the room chaotic or too noisy, or were things moving too slowly at circle time?

Then it is important to observe and record the **consequences**. Did the other children laugh at the child? Did the teacher reprimand the child? Recording the consequences is difficult because it may require teachers to reflect on their own actions. For example, if a teacher rushes to a child who is pushing another child off a chair, they may be reinforcing the pushing—that is, if the child is pushing in order to get the teacher's attention.

Program leaders can help teachers learn to observe by talking with them about ways they feel might work, such as keeping a pen and a small pad in their pocket to jot down a few notes right after the child calms down and before they forget what happened, or using their phone to record their impressions later. In this manner, they can also capture valuable information about the behavior's trigger and response.

Teachers should also be observing and recording times when the child is behaving appropriately so that they know what engages the child, when and where the child functions best, and who the child enjoys being with. This information will be key when it comes time to build the positive behavior support plan.

Developing a Hypothesis

In addition, teachers should participate fully in the next phase of the FA procedure: using all the data they have collected so far to work with the team to develop a hypothesis—a possible explanation or theory about the behavior's function or purpose. The hypothesis will become the foundation for the team's behavior support plan (O'Neill et al. 2015).

Creating a Behavior Support Plan

Once the team has identified the behavior, the antecedents, and the consequences and figured out the behavior's function or purpose, they are ready to construct a behavior support plan. They will need as many ideas and points of view as possible, so everyone on the team should participate, just as they did when they were working out the function of the behavior.

The child will resist efforts to change their behavior unless the replacement behavior is as efficient and effective as the problem behavior, so the plan should identify how the behavior can be prevented, the skills that the child needs to learn, and the responses that will encourage the child to meet their needs appropriately. It is also important to keep the child's positive moments, strengths, and interests clearly in mind (Dunlap et al. 2006).

Prevention

Begin by thinking about specific ways to prevent the challenging behavior. This will entail finding and changing its antecedents in the classroom environment—in the physical space, activities, curriculum, routines, and even the teacher's own behavior, words, and expectations. It can be as simple as getting several more popular trucks and dolls, controlling numbers by placing fewer chairs at an activity table, and offering different ways for children to complete a task so that if they are uncomfortable finger painting, they can use a brush (or vice versa). For an example of what this looks like, see "Ryan's A-B-C Observation Chart" on page 105.

Replacement Behaviors

Next the team must decide which skills the child needs to learn and how they will help the child replace their inappropriate behavior with appropriate behavior. Enabling the child to use an appropriate replacement behavior is the major goal. What can the child do that serves the same purpose? What skills do they have to learn? This inevitably involves teaching (O'Neill et al. 2015). Perhaps the most common skills a child with challenging behavior needs to learn are how to ask for help and how to ask for a break, but the possibilities are many and various. They may require help with joining a group, with throwing and catching a ball, with managing anger, or with finding a quiet space or a way to reduce their anxiety when they feel overwhelmed. The team should identify the steps required for the child to learn the new skill and start by choosing a skill that is easy to learn, preferably one based on the child's strengths, so that they will quickly experience success.

Responses to the Child's Behavior

The team must also select responses to use when the child behaves appropriately and when they behave inappropriately. If the function of the behavior is to obtain attention, the team must remember that the child's need for attention is very real, and they must provide the child with attention when the child is acting appropriately (but not when they are acting inappropriately).

What form will this positive reinforcement take? Again, the teachers must focus on what the child enjoys and is good at and figure out how they will make extra time to talk and play with the child. For example, if the child likes puzzles, the teacher might decide to spend special time with them at the puzzle table. If they enjoy cooking or baking, the teacher can create a cake-making project where the child can act as the first assistant chef. Or the teacher can plan to play with them and their beloved trucks or trains or bank time with them (Driscoll & Pianta 2010; Spiegel 2012).

Working out ways to deal with the child's inappropriate behavior will probably be much more difficult because the team must respond without rewarding the behavior. In cases where the function of the behavior (such as pushing) is to obtain attention, they can plan to ignore it and choose a different response (such as talking first to the child being pushed).

The team will need a different strategy when the child is trying to avoid something. Removing the child from the situation would reward challenging behavior, so the plan should not offer that possibility. Instead it is crucial to focus on factors in the immediate environment so that the team can figure out which ones trigger the behavior and how to change them. In such a situation, the teacher must support the child. For example, Carmen has difficulty sitting and listening at story time and often pinches or hits the children nearby. To encourage her to participate, the teacher can make sure Carmen has worry beads or a stress ball to hold or invite Carmen to sit beside her, turn the pages of the book, or even choose the story. These solutions may look like prevention, but of course they are preventive strategies and responses at the same time.

Last but not least, the plan should outline a method and timeline for evaluating progress.

Ryan's A-B-C Observation Chart

Child's Name: Ryan					
Date	Activity/teacher	Antecedent	Behavior	Maintaining consequence	Possible function
Monday, Dec. 11	Circle/Latoya	Starting a new song	Kicks, pinches child beside him	Told to keep hands to himself	Attention from teacher
		Everyone is singing	Pinches and hits child beside him	Told to leave circle and look at a book. He leaves	Escape from activity
	Getting ready to go outside/ Latoya	Struggling with his shoes	Throws shoes across the room	Teacher picks up the shoes and offers her help	Attention from teacher
	Gross motor hopping and jumping across the yard	Everyone is getting a turn in small groups	Yells and pushes Jon	Teacher removes him from group to sit and watch	Escape from activity
Thursday, Dec. 14	Art activity/ Latoya	Starting work, looks around at other children's work	Dumps the glue on the table and pushes his chair over	Teacher removes him from the activity	Escape from activity
	Storytime/Mike	Teacher starts reading	Gets up on his knees so other children cannot see	Teacher tells him to sit down	Attention from teacher
Friday, Dec. 15	Arrival/Maya	Other children involved in a variety of activities	Walks to block area and knocks over structure	Children yell at him	Attention from peers
	Circle time/ Latoya	Playing "Bug in a Rug"	Hits child beside him	Teacher asks him to leave circle. He leaves	Escape from activity
	Lunch time/ Latoya	Teacher reminds him that it is his turn to pour the milk	Pushes over his chair and kicks it	Teacher places him at a table by himself with his lunch and a glass of milk	Escape from pouring the milk

What Happens Next?

Teachers and program leaders should be aware that as soon as they change their responses to the child's challenging behavior, it is likely to get worse. This phenomenon is known as an *extinction burst*, and it will pass. In addition, it may take up to six weeks for them to see the results of their efforts, especially if the challenging behavior has been part of the child's repertoire for a long time. Teachers can start by concentrating on small improvements that they may need a leader's input to notice, such as that the child is using more positive behavior or that outbursts are shorter, less frequent, or less violent.

Once again, an important reminder: start the FA and positive behavior support process well before staff members are burned out and demanding the child be asked to leave the program. A child's challenging behavior is sending them a message: the task at hand is too difficult; the child does not understand the expectations; the child needs their attention; the environment is too loud and chaotic. Of course, not all of the causes of challenging behavior are in the immediate environment, but it is helpful to look at the behavior in this way. If the teachers and leaders listen carefully to the child's message, they will be able to identify the skills the child needs to learn, and ultimately they will become better teachers. Most of all, they need to let go of any negative feelings they have about the child's behavior and start fresh every day.

Reflection Questions

1. How do different team members contribute to the behavioral support planning process? How are the perspectives of teachers and families incorporated? Why are they important?

2. Who will conduct the functional assessment (FA) in your environment?

3. How might you consider the influence of a child's context (e.g., culture, language, abilities, experiences) on developing a behavior support plan?

4. How does team capacity impact intervention implementation?

FA offers significant clues to challenging behavior, but it is important to remember that it is not a cure-all, and behaviors may have more than one function. It helps program leaders and teachers to understand the importance of looking at the behavior from the child's point of view. If they can bolster the child's competence and confidence in one area, then other behaviors may become preventable or even cease completely.

REFERENCES

Bijou, S.W., R.F. Peterson, & M.H. Ault. 1968. "A Method to Integrate Descriptive and Experimental Field Studies at the Level of Data and Empirical Concepts." *Journal of Applied Behavior Analysis* 1 (2): 175–91.

Driscoll, K.C., & R.C. Pianta. 2010. "Banking Time in Head Start: Early Efficacy of an Intervention Designed to Promote Supportive Teacher-Child Relationships." *Early Education and Development* 21 (1): 38–64.

Dunlap, G., P.S. Strain, L. Fox, J.J. Carta, M. Conroy, B.J. Smith, L. Kern, M.L. Hemmeter, M.A. Timm, A. Mccart, W. Sailor, U. Markey, D.J. Markey, S. Lardieri, & C. Sowell. 2006. "Prevention and Intervention with Young Children's Challenging Behavior: Perspectives Regarding Current Knowledge." *Behavioral Disorders* 32 (1): 29–45.

Fox, L., & M.A. Duda. 2015. "Positive Behavior Support." Technical Assistance Center on Social Emotional Intervention for Young Children. https://researchgate.net/profile/Michelle-Duda/publication/299461771_Complete_Guide_to_Positive_Behavior_Support-Young_Children/links/56f9adfe08ae95e8b6d4031f/Complete-Guide-to-Positive-Behavior-Support-Young-Children.pdf.

Karsh, K.G., A.C. Repp, C.M. Dahlquist, & D. Munk. 1995. "In Vivo Functional Assessment and Multi-Element Interventions for Problem Behavior of Students with Disabilities in Classroom Settings." *Journal of Behavioral Education* 5 (2): 189–210.

O'Neill, R.E., R.W. Albin, K. Storey, R.H. Horner, & J.R. Sprague. 2015. *Functional Assessment and Program Development for Problem Behavior: A Practical Handbook.* 3rd ed. Stamford, CT: Cengage Learning.

Samuels, C.A. 2013. "Tensions Accompany Growth of PBIS Discipline Model." *Education Week*, August 27. https://edweek.org/ew/articles/2013/08/28/2pbis_ep.h33.html.

Spiegel, A. 2012. "Teachers' Expectations Can Influence How Students Perform." Health, September 17. National Public Radio. https://npr.org/sections/health-shots/2012/09/18/161159263/teachers-expectations-can-influence-how-students-perform.

About the Authors

Barbara Kaiser is the coauthor of *Challenging Behavior in Young Children* and *Meeting the Challenge.* She has over 40 years of experience working with young children, educators, and families. She has taught at Acadia University in Nova Scotia and at Concordia University and College Marie-Victorin in Montreal, Canada, and has provided workshops and keynotes on challenging behavior throughout the world.

Judy Sklar Rasminsky is a freelance writer who specializes in education and health. With coauthor Barbara Kaiser, she has written *Challenging Behavior in Young Children* (now in its fourth edition) and *Challenging Behavior in Elementary and Middle School*, which both earned Texty awards from the Text and Academic Authors Association; and *Meeting the Challenge*, a bestseller selected as a comprehensive membership benefit by NAEYC. For more information, see the authors' website, www.challengingbehavior.com, and blog, www.childrenwithchallengingbehavior.com.

This article is excerpted and adapted from B. Kaiser and J.S. Rasminsky, *Addressing Challenging Behavior in Young Children: The Leader's Role* (Washington, DC: NAEYC, 2021).

Photographs: pp. 100, 106 © Getty Images

Reducing Challenging Behavior During Transitions

Strategies for Early Childhood Educators to Share with Parents

Anne M. Butler and Michaelene M. Ostrosky

At pickup time, Teresa approaches her daughter's preschool teacher, Ms. Ann. Teresa would like some advice on how she can get her daughter, Lily, to transition more easily between daily activities. The previous evening, Lily had a tantrum at the end of library story time; she wanted to stay at the library longer, looking at picture books, but it was time to go home for dinner. Ms. Ann listens to Teresa and struggles to come up with concrete ideas for making outings such as these smoother for everyone.

Transitions are when children move from one activity to another. Everyday transitions include arriving at an educational setting from home, moving from dinner to playtime, finishing playtime and cleaning up, brushing teeth and then taking a bath, and going from bath time to bedtime. Transitions can be difficult for some parents, particularly when taking their young children out into the community (such as Teresa's struggles with Lily at the library), picking them up from educational settings, or moving between activities and routines at home. For some children, transitions may be frustrating or may provoke anxiety, and they may lead to challenging behavior. In this article, we adopt the definition of "challenging behavior" provided by the Center on Social and Emotional Foundations for Early Learning (CSEFEL; 2013):

> Any repeated pattern of behavior that interferes with learning or engagement in pro-social interactions with peers and adults.

> Behaviors that are not responsive to the use of developmentally appropriate guidance procedures.

> Prolonged tantrums, physical and verbal aggression, disruptive vocal and motor behavior (e.g., screaming, stereotypy), property destruction, self-injury, noncompliance, and withdrawal.

When young children engage in persistent challenging behavior, parents might look to their children's teachers for advice. The purpose of this article is to highlight strategies that early childhood educators can share with families in an effort to prevent challenging behavior during routine activities both inside and outside the home. We start with a discussion of why transitions may be difficult and when frustrations are most likely to occur. We then focus on the importance of early childhood professionals being knowledgeable about transition issues and offer suggestions and guidance for family members. Finally, we share strategies parents can use prior to and during transitions to prevent challenging behavior, as well as skills children can be taught to help make transitions easier.

Understanding the Difficulty of Transitions

Difficulty with transitions can occur for a number of reasons, such as when children are tired, hungry, confused, or not ready to end an activity. Difficulty with transitions is also common when children have communication delays, limited social and emotional skills, or intellectual disabilities (Hemmeter, Ostrosky, & Corso 2012). By considering children's needs and abilities and planning accordingly, parents can avoid problems at transition times. For example, instead of racing from one errand to another on a Saturday morning, parents might plan a 20-minute break to play with their children between stops. Early childhood educators can encourage parents to *put themselves in their children's shoes* and look at the world from their vantage points as they consider how to show their children what to do ("Leo, put the washcloth like this to scrub your legs"); how to keep their children busy ("Alex, while we wait for the server to bring our food, why don't we look at these books we brought along?"); and how to prepare their children for what comes next ("Jade, after we go to the bank, we will stop by the park for some crackers and juice and play on the slide for a bit").

Ideally, educators will customize these strategies as they get to know each family. Many parents struggle with transitions throughout a child's early years, so sharing strategies that might prevent challenging behavior during these times is an important task for early childhood educators. While some beginning educators report that they do not view parents as equal partners in family-centered practices and that working with parents can be difficult (Bezdek, Summers, & Turnbull 2010), parents often look to professionals for suggestions about how to address particular issues. Additionally, recommended practices in early childhood special education highlight the important role that parents play as partners in their children's learning and development (DEC 2014).

To be supportive—and to improve transitions at the beginning and end of each school day—early childhood educators should devote time to developing strategies to share with parents on successfully navigating transitions at home and in the community. "Given that challenging behavior has an impact on children as well as families, understanding challenging behavior in the context of families is critical" (Tyrrell, Freeman, & Chambers 2006, 30). For example, educators might collaborate with parents in deciding what strategy to try first to tackle a difficult transition. A teacher might say to a parent, "It seems Jack does better during long periods of waiting when he knows what will happen next and when he has something to play with. You mentioned that he often has a tantrum when you are both waiting at the bus stop for your third grader to come home. How do you think Jack would react if you brought a toy along, played a guessing game with him, or sang some songs?"

Helping with Transitions

There are several things that can be done to make potentially difficult transition times easier for parents and children. First, preventive strategies reduce the likelihood that transitions will be difficult or that challenging behavior will occur. Second, early childhood educators and parents can work together to determine how to teach children the skills needed to make transition times successful. Finally, there are specific individualized strategies that can be used when a transition becomes difficult or when a child's behavior escalates. These topics are discussed in the following sections.

Preventive Strategies

Early childhood educators may share ideas with parents about how to create smooth transitions at home, thereby decreasing the likelihood of challenging behavior occurring. While these ideas should be adapted to meet the needs of individual children, general strategies (Artman-Meeker & Kinder 2014) to share with family members include

> **Looking carefully at a family's schedule, routines, and transitions.** Help families think about (1) whether there are transitions or parts of routines that may not be necessary or that could be changed; (2) if their daily schedule could be more consistent, making it easier for children to predict the day; and (3) what strategies they could use to signal to their children that a transition is coming. For example, some families put a child-friendly schedule (with pictures to represent activities) on the refrigerator.

> **Planning ahead.** Have materials and activities on hand to transform wait time into fun learning time. For example, when standing in a long line at a store or when driving in the car, play I Spy to find objects that are a particular color or begin with a specific sound. Have quiet toys to use while waiting, such as word puzzles, books, or crayons and a coloring book.

> **Having materials ready.** Gather all necessary items for the next activity before signaling a transition to your child. For example, have the bath ready, shoes gathered, or apples out for snack time prior to calling a child to the activity.

> **Using music, songs, or predictable noises to signal transitions**. A routine cleanup song can be used when it is time to pick up toys. Set a timer to indicate that playtime is ending and soon it will be time to clean up for dinner.

> **Using visual cues.** Mini-schedules posted near transition locations provide visual prompts for the next transition or schedule change. For instance, picture cues near the front door might contain photos of a coat, hat, and boots to prompt a child to get ready to go outside.

> **Turning transition times into games.** Create a song and dance or engage in pretend play about what a child is going to do next. For example, children can be encouraged to "fly" to the sink like superheroes to brush their teeth.

The main goal of preventive strategies is to help children understand adults' expectations for transitions so that challenging behavior is less likely to occur (Hemmeter et al. 2008).

Skills to Teach

While preventive strategies are helpful, over time children need to learn to regulate their emotions and behaviors so that transitions are no longer difficult. Educators can provide parents with suggestions for specific skills to teach children. Even if parents have consistent, predictable routines in place and children know what is expected during transitions, challenging behavior may occur when a child does not have the necessary skills to complete the tasks someone is asking of them. It is important to collaborate with parents so that children develop specific skills needed during problematic transitions.

Consider the following:

> Ask parents to think about difficult transitions throughout the day, and encourage them to consider if their children have the necessary skills for understanding directions and moving to the next activity when a transition is signaled. For example, a parent may ask, "Does my child know how to brush their teeth independently, or do they need assistance?" "What might I do, or what skills might I teach my child, to assist them in getting dressed? In cleaning up before bedtime?"

> Suggest that parents practice skills with their children and provide descriptive feedback on how their children use those skills. For example, a child may be able to put their coat on but might not know how to zip or button it. Parents can (1) provide descriptive feedback once the child puts on their coat ("You put your coat on all by yourself!"); (2) show the child how to zip or button the coat and encourage them to help ("I know the zipper can be hard, so how about I hold the bottom of your coat

and then help you zip it?" [Meadan et al. 2013]); (3) provide praise or descriptive feedback once essential tasks have been completed and add a cue for the transition to begin ("I like that you put on your hat and gloves all by yourself after we zipped your coat! I can tell you are ready to go to the store now"); and (4) give feedback once the child makes the transition ("You did a great job getting into your car seat. Now we can go to the pet store").

> Encourage parents to teach their children a variety of emotion words so they can express their feelings. Sometimes children have an easier time making difficult transitions when they are able to communicate their desires and emotions. For example, when a child is upset about leaving the park, an adult can label this emotion by saying, "It looks like you are upset about leaving the park. Are you upset? Would you like to tell me why you are upset about leaving?" After pausing to see if the child responds, the parent could continue, "I am upset about leaving the park. I like playing here with you. We need to go now because it's dinnertime. If the weather is nice tomorrow, we can come back."

> Brainstorm with parents some strategies for teaching children problem solving skills so they learn to come up with alternative solutions to situations that arise. For example, a parent might ask a child, "What do you want to quietly play with while we take grandpa to the doctor's office?" Such questions help children consider variables like, "This toy makes music, so I can't bring it." Another useful strategy is a four-step problem solving process (CSEFEL 2013), in which parents ask their children to consider the following: (1) What is the problem?; (2) Think, think, think of some solutions; (3) What would happen if we tried the solution? Would it be fair? Would it be safe? How would everyone feel?; and (4) Give the solution a try! Through this process, children learn to problem solve with guidance and support.

> Encourage parents to use "First . . ., then . . ." statements to communicate their expectations and to help children learn to wait patiently for preferred activities. For instance, a parent might say, "First you need to put the books on the shelf, and then you can play outside."

Individualized Strategies

Even with preventive strategies in place and efforts made to teach new skills, there will still be times when transitions are challenging for some children. By learning about the specific situations that remain difficult, early childhood educators can provide parents with individualized suggestions. For example, if a child regularly has trouble with the transition from school to the car during pickup time, a teacher might give the child clear directions in the presence of the parent, describing to the child exactly what behaviors they expect to see as they walk to the car ("Shannon, I need to see walking feet and gentle hands as we walk to the car with Mom."). Early childhood educators also might model transition behaviors for the child while the parent is present ("Shannon, watch me walk to the cubbies, take out your backpack, and help you put it on to go home.").

Preventive strategies and new skills might not work well if parents have a hard time remaining warm and supportive when their children act out. The importance of remaining calm during difficult transitions cannot be overemphasized. Educators can offer suggestions to parents about how to develop their own cooldown strategies during stressful times (such as counting to 10 and visualizing a calming place). Educators can also help parents learn to redirect their children as a way to defuse a difficult transition. For example, as Cameron begins fussing about not wanting to take off his new snow boots, Ms. Annette might say, "We got some new fish in the fish tank today; we'll go check them out as soon as your boots are off."

Supporting Parents

Some parents may seek support from educators or ask questions about a particular incident or transition, while other parents may have difficulty with multiple transitions. It is critical that educators consider which strategies best meet parents' unique needs. While educators should model for parents when opportunities arise, educators should also plan for less stressful learning opportunities during which they problem solve with parents. Some suggestions for sharing ideas with parents follow.

Parent Workshops

Parent workshops can provide wonderful learning opportunities on creating successful transitions, while also allowing parents to see that they are not alone. During group workshops, early educators can cover topics such as preventive strategies, how to teach children the necessary skills to be successful during transitions, and how to manage challenging behavior during transitions (for example, see the National Center for Pyramid Model Innovations [NCPMI] Positive Solutions for Families parent training modules at www.challengingbehavior.org/document/positive-solutions-for-families-sessions-1-7). During parent workshops, educators can demonstrate strategies for parents, role-play, and share information regarding how school transitions are structured. Videos of difficult transitions could be used as a foundation for collaboratively developing solutions. (For example, a video showing a transition using a timer can be found at www.vimeo.com/194715303, while a video depicting transition cues can be viewed at www.vimeo.com/194715224. For even more video examples, visit https://bit.ly/2JDYBz2.)

Home Communication

Proactively communicating with parents about transitions is another strategy that early childhood educators can use to maintain positive connections between school and home. For example, a monthly newsletter with transition tips can be sent home to parents, or weekly transition ideas can be inserted into a classroom newsletter. Additionally, communication logs can be created for individual children. These logs go between home and school as a method of sharing information with parents who would like support or suggestions for specific transitions. This provides an opportunity for educators and parents to learn about which strategies are successful at school and home, generate ideas for individual children, and examine challenges that continue to occur.

Transition Resources

Routines and Schedules

From the NCPMI Backpack Connection Series:

> "How to Help Your Child Have a Successful Morning" www.challengingbehavior.org/docs/backpack/BackpackConnection_routines_morning.pdf

> "How to Help Your Child Have a Successful Bedtime" www.challengingbehavior.org/docs/backpack/BackpackConnection_routines_bedtime.pdf

> "How to Use Visual Schedules to Help Your Child Understand Expectations" www.challengingbehavior.org/docs/backpack/BackpackConnection_routines_visual-schedules.pdf

> "How to Help Your Child Transition Smoothly Between Places and Activities" www.challengingbehavior.org/docs/backpack/BackpackConnection_routines_transitions.pdf

From ZERO TO THREE:

> "Creating Routines for Love and Learning" www.zerotothree.org/resource/creating-routines-for-love-and-learning

Encouragement for Successful Transitions

From the National Center for Pyramid Model Innovations:

> "Some Starters for Giving Positive Feedback and Encouragement" www.challengingbehavior.org/docs/ToolsBuildingRelationships_starters-for-giving-positive-feedback.pdf

Reflection Questions

1. What might be some important transitions for the families of children you teach? How are they similar to or different from the classroom transitions you guide children through?

2. What might be some challenges families face during transitions at home?

3. Thinking about similarities and differences between transitions at home and in the early learning program setting, what are a few strategies that might work in one place but not the other? Why? What are a few strategies that can work in both settings?

Observations and Modeling

If children are struggling with transition times, parents can observe educators modeling strategies during classroom transitions. Some parents may benefit from paying attention to the expectations and directions teachers provide and then watching how their children react during the transition. This sort of modeling could be done while a parent is volunteering in the classroom, on a field trip with the class, or attending a parent night. Additionally, some parents might benefit from educators coaching them as they learn new strategies for supporting their children during difficult transitions. This might involve educators sharing detailed information on steps to follow when preparing for a transition, as well as performance-based feedback on what worked well and what a parent might do differently next time.

Conclusion

When early childhood educators and family members collaborate to support children who struggle with transitions, everyone benefits. Teachers and parents should communicate about their difficulties with transitions to determine possible solutions, like Ms. Ann does with Teresa in this closing vignette.

A few days after Teresa asks Ms. Ann for help making transitions easier for Lily, Ms. Ann shares a few strategies she uses in the classroom when challenging behavior arises. She suggests three strategies: trying "First . . ., then . . ." statements to establish expectations, modeling emotion words so Lily can talk about her feelings, and helping Lily think about what might make her feel better.

Teresa thanks Ms. Ann and decides to try these strategies at the library that evening. "First we will go to story time at the library, then we will drive home to eat dinner," Teresa says to Lily as they get ready to go to the library. After story time,

Teresa reminds Lily that it is time to go home for dinner. Lily starts to become upset, and Teresa worries that she's going to have another tantrum. Remembering Ms. Ann's advice, she asks, "Are you sad we have to leave the library? Can you tell me why you're sad?" Lily says she wants more story time. Teresa asks her if she would like to do story time at home. She explains that they can borrow the same book that they just heard during story time and read it over and over at home. Lily nods enthusiastically. Together, they take the book to the library checkout desk, calm and happy.

REFERENCES

Artman-Meeker, K., & K. Kinder. 2014. "Moving Right Along: Planning Transitions to Prevent Challenging Behavior." Front Porch Series Broadcast Calls. Head Start Early Childhood Learning & Knowledge Center, The National Center on Quality Teaching and Learning. Video. https://eclkc.ohs.acf.hhs.gov/video/planning-transitions-prevent-challenging-behavior.

Bezdek, J., J.A. Summers, & A. Turnbull. 2010. "Professionals' Attitudes on Partnering with Families of Children and Youth with Disabilities." *Education and Training in Autism and Developmental Disabilities* 45 (3): 356–65.

CSEFEL (Center on the Social and Emotional Foundations for Early Learning). 2013. "Module 3a, Individualized Intensive Interventions: Determining the Meaning of Challenging Behavior." http://csefel.vanderbilt.edu/resources/training_preschool.html.

DEC (Division for Early Childhood of the Council for Exceptional Children). 2014. "DEC Recommended Practices in Early Intervention/Early Childhood Special Education." www.dec-sped.org/recommendedpractices.

Hemmeter, M.L., M.M. Ostrosky, K.M. Artman, & K.A. Kinder. 2008. "Moving Right Along . . . Planning Transitions to Prevent Challenging Behavior." *Young Children* 63 (3): 18–25.

Hemmeter, M.L., M.M. Ostrosky, & R.M. Corso. 2012. "Preventing and Addressing Challenging Behavior: Common Questions and Practical Strategies." *Young Exceptional Children* 15 (2): 32–46.

Meadan, H., M.M. Ostrosky, R.M. Santos, & M.R. Snodgrass. 2013. "How Can I Help? Prompting Procedures to Support Children's Learning." *Young Exceptional Children* 16 (4): 31–39.

Tyrrell, A.L., R. Freeman, & C.R. Chambers. 2006. "Family Perceptions of Challenging Behavior: Strategies for Providing Effective Supports." In *Young Exceptional Children Monograph Series No. 8: Supporting Social Emotional Development in Young Children*, eds. E.M. Horn & H. Jones, 29–41. Missoula, MT: Division for Early Childhood of the Council for Exceptional Children.

About the Authors

Anne M. Butler, PhD, is assistant professor in the department of Counseling and Special Education at DePaul University, Chicago. Her research focuses on collaborating with teachers and families to implement strategies around challenging behavior and the practical application of those strategies in classrooms.

Michaelene M. Ostrosky, PhD, is Grayce Wicall Gauthier professor of education in the department of Special Education at the University of Illinois Urbana-Champaign. Throughout her career, she has been involved in research and dissemination of findings on the inclusion of children with disabilities, social and emotional competence, and challenging behavior.

Index

Page numbers followed by *b, f,* and *t* indicate text boxes, figures, and tables, respectively.